REPTILAND

Reticulated python circa 1984. L to R: Whitney Peeling, Elliot Peeling, Chad Peeling, Dianne Peeling, Michael McDevitt, Clyde Peeling, Dave Osman, Clair Thompson. Photo courtesy Terry Wild.

REPTILAND

How a Boyhood Dream became a Modern Zoo

Clyde Peeling

Published in the United States by Peeling Productions
www.peelingproductions.com

Library of Congress Cataloging-in-Publication Data
Clyde Peeling 1942—

Reptiland: How a Boyhood Dream became a Modern Zoo
/Clyde Peeling
132 p. cm.

1. Autobiography. I Title.

ISBN 978-0-9960790-0-6

PRINTED IN THE UNITED STATES OF AMERICA

Book design by Whitney Peeling and Christian Steinbacher

Cover design by Christian Steinbacher

Second Edition

To the hundreds of employees, friends, and family, without whose efforts my dream could not have been realized.

Acknowledgements

This book would never have come to fruition had my daughter Whitney not insisted I stay with it and finish the project. Whitney, a publicist in the publishing industry, also selected many of the photos from family and business archives and offered valuable advice. Many other people provided indispensible help. My friend, Debbie Behler, past editor of *Wildlife Conservation* magazine and co-author of *Frogs: A Chorus of Colors* and other publications, made valuable suggestions and corrections to the early manuscript. Jennie Erin Smith, author of *Stolen World*, *Cocaine Cowgirl*, and numerous magazine articles, helped with chronology. My wife, Dianne, made improvements as did our son Chad who ruthlessly cut superfluous and unnecessary sections. John Strawbridge, Richard Hahn, and Joe McDonald offered suggestions at various stages. Christian Steinbacher, graphic artist at Reptiland, helped with design and final layout. With such a wealth of talent the reader has every reason to expect an exceptional book but any shortcomings belong to me. As they say, "you can't make a peach out of a lemon."

TABLE OF CONTENTS

Foreword by John Strawbridge

Foreword

If, as Will Rogers said, "...all (you) know is what little news (you) read every day in the newspapers," you may have a distorted view of the life of our country. News reporting, almost by definition, is focused on the negative, especially on the antics of government officials and so-called celebrities. We are often told what people *say* they do, rather than what they *actually* do–hyperbole supplants reality. Yet, in a national population of more than 300 million, there are many untold stories which define us as a people: tales of survival and achievement, of family, community, and enterprise. Most of our personal lives have included hardship and misfortune, but the outcome often has been positive. One of those stories is the subject of this memoir. I can vouch for its honesty because I was there for the duration, as a friend.

Though conceived in a small town in Pennsylvania, Clyde Peeling pretty much assembled himself as he went along, assimilating a broader view of the world than his birthright demanded. He claims to be a composite of everybody he's ever met, and that may be true. But the reverse is also true. Those of us who know him have been influenced by his positive nature and determination to never give up. Once he decides to do something, he perseveres until he accomplishes it, however long it takes, however many voices tell him it can't be done. The existence of Reptiland is proof of this unwillingness to accept failure.

Fascinated by reptiles as a boy, Clyde has single-mindedly pursued that interest ever since. He grew up in the age of roadside menageries, yet his intellectual growth and hard work resulted in the creation of a specialized zoological park held in high esteem by visitors and zoo professionals alike. Society's view of captive animals has changed dramatically over our lifetimes and Reptiland has done what few other private zoos have—it has evolved from a place centered on public amusement and recreation to an educational institution and an important force for the conservation of the natural world.

Development of Reptiland involved the challenges of financial management, design and construction, and animal husbandry. But it also involved assembling a community of people who could bring ideas to fruition, lend support and encouragement, and help modernize the vision. Clyde is a gregarious character. In addition to the Reptiland staff, his community of supporters has included colleagues at some of America's finest zoos and aquariums; academic scientists and philosophers; environmentalists and business people; and eccentric, bright individuals from many other walks of life. The most important supporters have been Clyde's wife, Dianne; their daughter, Whitney; their two sons, Elliot and Chad; and their daughter-in-law, Chris.

Reptiland is more than a personal triumph of its founder. It is an institution that has played an important role in changing public attitudes toward reptiles. At its beginning 50 years ago, reptiles were viewed with an almost biblical hatred—remembering Eve and the serpent—and snakes were killed on sight. Now, thanks to nature programming on television, environmental education, and the influence of zoos, there has been a major shift toward appreciation of once-maligned creatures. Lizards, snakes, crocodilians, and turtles are now seen, particularly by young people, as valuable threads in the network of life on earth.

As you read this book you will learn that private aviation is another of Clyde's passions. I was with him one clear night not long ago, flying south from Pennsylvania along the chain of the Appalachians, a canopy of stars above, and a scattering of lights below in almost every valley and up the mountain slopes. Curmudgeon that I am, my thoughts were about the fragmentation of the American forest, the impacts of population growth, of mining and other threats to biodiversity. By contrast, Clyde looked around on this beautiful night and said, "I'm really glad to be a part of all this." I'm glad he is, too.

John Strawbridge
Inverness, Florida 2014

CHAPTER 1
I'm Going to Build a Zoo

MY HIGH SCHOOL GUIDANCE COUNSELOR held my report card in his hand, examining my grades with concern. He looked up at me and asked, in a gravely serious tone, what I intended to do with my life. I'm going to build a reptile zoo, I told him. That might be fine as a hobby, but how, he wanted to know, did I intend to make a living? He refused to take me seriously and assured me that unless my grades improved, I would find myself without a means of support. He was right about my grades of course, and, more than once over the years, I wondered if he'd been right about my career choice. But I wasn't about to let him or a host of other naysayers think they had been correct. I was determined to build my zoo, and failure was not an option I seriously contemplated.

What I lacked in knowledge—in short, everything—I made up for in confidence and determination. And I had an extremely supportive family. I realize now that naiveté is probably a prerequisite for anyone starting a business with no financial capital and very little experience. With full knowledge of the pitfalls that lay ahead, no rational person would plunge in. Certainly they wouldn't be foolish enough to build a zoo. But that's exactly what I did.

John Lennon said, 'Life is what happens while you're busy making other plans." This book is about the successes, failures, near disasters, transformation of philosophy, and unforeseen pitfalls that threatened to derail the fulfillment of my dream. The zoo that exists along the highway in central Pennsylvania today is far better than the zoo I dreamed of building more than five decades ago. And, it's not only the zoo that's changed; I am not the same person I was at the beginning of the journey. Life just happens.

CHAPTER 2
Born a Dreamer

AS A CHILD I WAS, like many kids, fascinated by reptiles. Unlike a lot of kids, whose parents drew the line at having a snake in the house, I was encouraged to pursue my interest—and to believe I could do anything I set my mind to so long as I worked tirelessly at it. I was born July 10, 1942, in Muncy, Pennsylvania. My parents named me Clyde Robert. Clyde, after my grandfather on my mother's side, and Robert, because, according to my father, there had always been a Robert in the Peeling side of the family. Everyone called me Bob until I entered the United States Air Force.

My mother, Charlotte Foust, grew up on a rural farm in central Pennsylvania within walking distance of the village of Clarkstown, where I spent most of my early childhood. She worked hard all her life. When my brother Don and I were very young, she dug a basement beneath our house to make room for a new furnace. Every day she carried dirt from under the house, one bucket-full at a time. Each spring, a few weeks before Easter, she made chocolate-dipped peanut butter and coconut eggs, which she sold to families up and down the street to make extra money. My job was grating the coconut meat, and she bought me my first suit with the proceeds. She loved gardening and tried her best to pass that love on to her children. It took with my brother Don, who loves to grow a garden. I, on the other hand, hated picking out rocks, pulling weeds, and harvesting vegetables. I decided very early that I wanted no part of farming or gardening.

My father, George Carlton Peeling, was a gunsmith and machinist. When I was young, he operated a small shop just two doors up the street from our house. Later, he went to work for Jones and Laughlin Steel Corporation. He headed the maintenance department of their wire rope division in Muncy—a larger community about four miles from Clarkstown. My fondest memories of him center on his machine shop. On cold winter days, the old-timers and unemployed young men home from World War II would cluster round the pot-bellied stove and shoot the breeze, while my dad worked at his lathe, drill press, or milling machine, repairing a gun or piece of farm equipment. In the early 1950s, before freezers were mass-produced, and no one in our town had one, he researched industrial versions and built his own, which everyone in town then used to store their perishables. He had a first rate mind for mechanics and always said he could "fix anything but a broken heart."

Though I often bristled against his overbearing nature, my father had a huge influence on me. I didn't inherit his mechanical skills, but he instilled in me a deep respect for innovation, a commitment to honesty, and a sense that I was special and could do anything I set my mind to. It is a little surprising that his message took. I was a mediocre student, lazy and disinterested in most subjects. In school I used whatever force of personality I had to squeak through each report card period.

Above all else, I was a dreamer. At one point I was interested in circuses and set about, together with my best friend Dick Williamson, to create the *Peeling and Williamson Brothers Circus.* We were not brothers, but I suppose we thought the name gave us more credibility, like *Cole Brothers* and *Ringling Brothers* circuses. I remember recruiting my younger brother, Don, and other kids around Clarkstown to be part of the show. One recruit's mother forced him into early retirement after he hurt his leg. He was to be our high diver, and I had encouraged him to leap into a shallow pool from atop a tall stepladder, which may have had something to do with the injury.

Because my father was a gunsmith, my brother and I grew up around firearms and spent a great deal of our youth shooting. Every fall my father took Don, Dick Williamson, and me to an annual sporting event along Loyalsock Creek. The highlight was exhibition shooting—one year by a husband-wife team, Dot and Ernie Lind; the following year by Herb Parsons. They were all expert marksmen with a flair for showmanship. We sat spellbound as they threw coin-size metal disks into the air, took aim, and not only hit each disk, but made it spin left or right by hitting one side or the other. Sometimes Herb Parsons would throw heads of cabbage into the air, making coleslaw as he hit each in rapid succession with his Winchester Model 12. I loved their entertaining patter and envisioned myself some day as a sharpshooter.

In my pre-teens I read a book about William F. Cody, "Buffalo Bill," and decided that a Wild West show would be my road to fame and fortune. Cody fired my imagination. He popularized the West, brought his version of it to Easterners and Europeans with his traveling show and, more than any other individual, shaped the popular vision of the early American West. Not consciously, but in many ways I think I patterned my life after Cody. I learned from him the usefulness of a public image, and later decided that snakes and other reptiles would be the Wild West that I would help popularize.

My friend Dick Williamson introduced me to snakes. Together we caught a common garter snake which I brought home and kept in our basement. I fed it small balls of raw hamburger by gently forcing open its mouth and inserting the meat, then carefully releasing my hold as the snake began to swallow on its own. It was not an ideal diet for a garter snake, which typically eats earthworms, frogs, and minnows. Nevertheless, the snake survived a remarkably long time.

My fascination with snakes grew, and at some point it occurred to me that I might make a career out of this passion. I talked with anyone I thought was an expert. Every summer my parents took me to the Lycoming County Fair in Hughesville. On the midway I discovered a sideshow that featured, among other attractions, a fire-eater who doubled as a human pincushion. To attract a crowd, he carried a beautiful eastern indigo snake on stage, while a barker extolled the wondrous freaks one could see inside the tent for the small fee of 25 cents. I convinced my dad to let me go in so I could meet the fellow with the snake.

His name was Wiley Everridge, and he cared about snakes and knew more than one might expect of a peripatetic carny. Before I could meet him, though, I had to endure his act. The fire eating was tolerable, but when he began to push old-fashioned foot-long hatpins through his arms, cheeks, and nose, I began to feel clammy. Perspiration beaded up on my forehead, and I came very close to fainting. Somehow I managed to hold it together until he finished. We soon became friends, and I visited Wiley at the fair each summer for a number of years.

I am not sure exactly when, but I decided early on—certainly before high school—that a reptile zoo was my future. My dad and, somewhat less enthusiastically, my mother supported my decision, but many adults thought it was an adolescent fantasy. Most, like my guidance counselor, thought it was completely unrealistic, but there were two teachers at Muncy High School who believed in me. I had begun high school on an academic track, but my lackluster grades forced me to take business courses instead. In those days the business track taught bookkeeping and shorthand skills, almost exclusively to girls. Our business teacher, Evelyn Yeagle, took a liking to me, though I didn't do particularly well in her classes. She knew about the reptile zoo idea. More important, she believed I would do it and must have seen a glimmer of promise in the only boy in her class. In her bookkeeping tests, she usually included a problem that involved my future zoo and me. I'm sure the girls in the class tired of her pandering to my strange interest, but they tolerated it and some even offered me after-school help before major exams. Evelyn knew how to play me, and I loved her, because she encouraged me and gave me confidence. Most adults seemed to enjoy telling me I was doomed to failure.

The other encouraging teacher was football coach Stan Schuyler, who taught typing and business law. I had no interest in football, but that didn't matter to Stan, who even came to my home after school one afternoon to help feed a northern copperhead. My parents allowed me to keep a few venomous species, but they had a firm rule that I could not handle them. The snake was not eating, and I was sure it would die of starvation if I didn't try something. Stan gently pinned the snake's head and picked it up so I could slide a dead mouse down its throat.

Scouting also provided opportunities to pursue my interest in reptiles. In the 1950s, the Boy Scouts of America seemed like a much more mainstream organization than it is today (sadly, its struggle to accept homosexuality and atheism has cooled my enthusiasm for it). Our small troop in Clarkstown did a lot of camping, and we caught crawfish, hellgrammites, wood turtles, hellbenders, and water snakes around Muncy Creek. When I was inducted into the Order of the Arrow—a national honor society of scouts—I learned the Hopi Indian hoop and snake dances. The hoop dance gave me special status, because I used five hoops instead of the traditional three, and finished with a single flaming hoop. But the snake dance— although requiring less skill—was the real crowd pleaser and led to my first experience with an exotic reptile. The Hopi Indians used rattlesnakes and believed dancing with them would help bring rain to their sun-parched soil. My father was adamant that I could not dance with live rattlesnakes, but he allowed me to order a boa constrictor, a harmless South American species, from a man named Ross Allen in Silver Springs, Florida.

This man's biography—*Adventures with Reptiles: The Story of Ross Allen*—had previously captured my imagination, and Ross had become my hero. Many kids my age, who were interested in reptiles, looked up to Ross Allen. In those days my parents never took Florida vacations, but I dreamed of someday visiting Ross's Reptile Institute and desperately wanted to be like him. Ross wore high, snake-proof boots tucked into riding breeches. I thought he looked dashing and, one Christmas, asked for a pair of Gokey snake boots—a very expensive set of footwear. On Christmas morning, I was disappointed to discover beneath the tree a pair of motorcycle boots about a third as high as Ross's Gokey boots. Many years later, as an adult on a trip to central Florida with my young family, I drove to Silver Springs and spent an afternoon with my boyhood hero, catching and loading large alligators into the back of a trailer.

My mail-ordered snake, a beautiful six-foot boa constrictor, arrived from Ross in 1956. In those days reptiles were shipped by railway express, so I waited nervously for the call that my snake had arrived. Rail was a rough way to transport live animals, and they sometimes were dead on arrival. On one occasion, I received an empty box with a note attached, explaining that a snake had escaped the box en route. But this, my first shipment, arrived intact, and the boa was in good health. It may not have been the species used by the Hopi Indians, but it impressed the audiences watching my Boy Scout dancing.

Every Wednesday night throughout the summer camping season, new kids were inducted into the Order of the Arrow. The event included American Indian dancing, and my parents drove me, once every week, to Camp Kline along Pennsylvania's Pine Creek, so I could take part in the ceremonies. And, every summer, I spent a week there with my troop. The camp nature lodge was run by Bob Mayer, who was about four years older than me. Known as "Snakey," because of his fondness for reptiles, Bob encouraged my interests.

In 1957 my parents sent me to the National Boy Scout Jamboree in Valley Forge, Pennsylvania, a significant commitment for them. We weren't poor, but there was never a lot of extra money. More than 50,000 scouts from all over the country descended on Valley Forge National Park, turning it into a sea of tented encampments. For the first time I met other kids interested in reptiles, and we traded live specimens: a common garter snake for a Texas horned lizard; an eastern painted turtle for a western bull snake. I continued to correspond with some of those kids for a number of years. One, Rick Hahn, became a lifelong friend.

Rick was born of solid German stock and grew up in Schnecksville, Pennsylvania, not far from Allentown. We visited each other every summer, and each of us aspired to build our own zoos. When I began Reptiland in 1964, Rick and his young wife, Mary Anne, periodically came to visit. A couple of years later they bought Jungleland Snake Farm, an existing zoo along Route 15, just south of the Pennsylvania border near Thurmont, Maryland. Gordon Gaver had owned Jungleland and, after he died, his widow sold the zoo to the Hahns. Rick renamed the establishment Catoctin Mountain Zoological Park and, more recently, Catoctin Wildlife Preserve and Park. Rick has a catholic interest in animals that extends well beyond reptiles, and his knowledge of exotic animals far exceeds my own. He's also a natural-born "horse trader" and built his zoo, in part, by constantly buying, selling, and trading animals with other zoos around the country.

CHAPTER 3
Early Mentors

IN THE LATE 1950S, Grit, a Sunday gazette with a national circulation published in Williamsport, ran a story about a tourist attraction called Reptiland, located along Route 15 near Winfield, Pennsylvania. I pleaded with my parents to take me there. Jim Travis, a handsome and charming Texan, owned it. In the summer of 1959, I went to work for him, giving guided tours to visitors.

Jim Travis was typical of many people in the animal business in those days. The animals were simply a way to make a living. It was generally believed that many reptile species could not be kept alive for long in captivity, and no one even considered breeding them. They were cheap and expendable. The ones that arrived alive lasted one, two, maybe three months and succumbed. Travis would then order replacements. My fellow tour guide, Dahle Bingaman, and I did not like that part of the business (Dahle said many years later, "the mindless destruction of so many beautiful animals was shameful. We placed blame on Travis, but in fairness, that was the state of the animal attraction industry at that time."). We were sure it could be done better and spent many long evenings, after closing time, discussing how we would do things differently if we owned Reptiland.

To our way of thinking, Travis was unwilling to put any financial resources back into the business. Maybe it was partially because he leased, rather than owned, the property but I suspect he really didn't care much for reptiles. Travis would periodically place an order for a $25, $50, or $100 "snake den"—a sort of mystery grab bag of various species. These usually came from the animal dealer Trudy Jerkins in Tarpon Springs, Florida. Trudy owned Tarpon Zoo with her partner Mike Tsalickis. Mike ran a compound in Leticia, Colombia, where he bought reptiles and other animals from indigenous people, then shipped them to Trudy, who sold them to carnivals and zoos. Nearly thirty years later, Mike was caught attempting to smuggle 7,300 pounds of cocaine inside cedar boards through the port of St. Petersburg, Florida and sentenced to 27 years in state prison.

One of the most valuable skills I acquired while working for Jim Travis was how to lecture—how to hold the attention of an audience; how to make people laugh; how to drive home my points. Although Travis was capable, I seldom learned much from him about public speaking. I learned more by emulating my co-worker, Dahle Bingaman, and by being thrust in front of visitors day after day. It was not unusual for us to give ten guided tours a day. I learned to look visitors in the eyes, enunciate, and speak loudly enough to be heard. The intensive practice honed my oratory skills, and the experience has served me well over the years. In spite of his faults, Travis had an irresistible charm for Dahle and me, and we still talk about it. It was through Travis that I met a number of people who would change the course of my life.

Travis's brother-in-law, J.G. "Bo" Miller, owned roadside zoos in Maggie Valley, North Carolina; Pigeon Forge, Tennessee; and Schroon Lake, New York. Travis often told stories about Bo and another man he had worked with—the veteran animal dealer, Arthur Jones. Although it would be a couple of years before I met either of them, Miller and Jones loomed larger than life in Travis's stories.

In the fall of 1960, at the end of the summer tourist season, Travis invited me to travel with him to his home in Jollyville, near Austin, Texas. We drove in his pickup to Maggie Valley, North Carolina and stayed the first night at Soco Reptile Gardens with another member of his family, Les Cowan. Les ran the Soco operation for Bo Miller. Soco had always been profitable, and I was told that, at the height of the summer tourist season, the place grossed $10,000 a week—a lot of money in those days. The prosperity of Soco may have reinforced my belief that I could someday make a living in the business.

Our next stop was Slidell, Louisiana. A hurricane had swept through Slidell a few days earlier, destroying many properties in the area, but Reptile Jungle, Arthur Jones' zoo, had weathered the storm without damage. His zoo was largely a series of stuccoed concrete pits to display snakes, lizards, and crocodilians. It was designed with aesthetic flair and by far the slickest private zoo I had ever seen. We spent the night with Arthur Jones. He was short, lean, and walked with his head bent slightly forward, unable to turn it from side to side—the result, I had been told, of an airplane accident. When Arthur entered a room he had everyone's attention. He spoke with complete authority in a deep gravelly voice with a slight Oklahoma twang, and people never questioned what he was saying—at least not to his face.

Arthur had a fascinating intensity about him, a fierceness of purpose. I was mesmerized. Although much of what he said sounded like braggadocio, I believed he could stand behind most of his claims. When we met, Arthur had already branched out from the animal business and was making wildlife films as well. He was producing a syndicated television series called *Wild Cargo* and in the process of editing *Voodoo Swamp*—a disastrous feature film that he laughed about years later. We sat in Arthur's editing room, and I listened as he and Travis talked well into the early morning hours. Arthur said he intended to make so much money he could tell the rest of the world to go f--- itself. He had two World War II surplus B-25s that he flew to South America, Asia, and Africa to capture and film wild animals. At age 18, I was impressed, and the idea must have occurred to me that I, too, might someday learn to fly.

From Slidell, Jim Travis and I continued west, past New Orleans, along the Gulf Coast to Houston, where we spent the night with Bo Miller and his wife Clara. It was just after Labor Day, and they had recently closed the New York Serpentarium, in the Adirondacks, for the season. I was immersed in talk of the zoo business and thrilled to be part of it. Like Arthur, Bo was a tough, charming character—a man's man. He had a checkered past. According to some members of the family, he had once gone to prison for robbing a bank. He had been identified by his voice, since he had worn a mask, but had never said a word during the robbery. They had the right guy despite the false testimony, and Bo served his time.

Bo had grown up in a circus family and gotten into grift zoos. A grift zoo was essentially a front for an illegal gambling operation. Arthur Jones explained to me years later how they functioned. Signs up and down the highway advertised a free zoo to travelers. When an expensive car pulled into the zoo parking lot, an experienced confidence man would strike up a conversation and attempt to lure the driver into a backroom, where he was given the opportunity to win big money. Of course the game was rigged, and he'd lose his shirt. If it seemed like the mark might become a problem, the owner of the grift zoo would follow his car. If the mark headed for the police station, the zoo owner would quickly pull him over and ask whether, by chance, he had lost any money during his visit at the zoo. When the fellow said that he not only lost money, but had been cheated, the owner would offer to return his money and thank the man, because he—the owner—had suspected something like that had been going on for some time. Most of the suckers didn't bother with the police, too ashamed to admit to their own stupidity.

Eventually Bo realized that people were interested in the animals—that the zoos could dispense with the gambling and support themselves through admissions alone. At his wife's insistence, Bo went legitimate. I found him to be kind, generous and a man of his word. I never had reason to think of him otherwise. He proved to be a good friend.

Jim Travis and I traveled on the next morning, finally arriving at his small stone house outside Austin. I spent a month there with Jim, his wife Barbara, and their four children, Ike, Wayne, and twins Justin and Joan. One weekend Travis and I drove down to Laredo and crossed the border into Mexico. It was my first of many forays into Mexico—a place I still find fascinating for its culture, rugged terrain, and wildlife.

CHAPTER 4
Texas to Greenland

I KNEW I HAD TO get my military obligation out of the way, as the choice in 1960 was either wait to be drafted or select a branch of the military and sign up. I decided to return to Pennsylvania by bus to enlist in the Air Force. On the way home, I managed to lose what little money I had to a con man during a stop in Oklahoma City. A perfect mark, I stepped off the bus dressed in new cowboy boots and Western duds. As I looked for a place to grab breakfast before catching a connecting bus to Pennsylvania, a friendly man approached and asked if I would join him for a bite at a café near the bus station. On our way there, another man staggered toward us, apparently drunk. In his hand was a thick wad of bills. He mumbled something about his sister, whom he said he hated, claimed it was her money, and asked if we wanted to flip a coin for it. My "friend" initially said we couldn't think of taking his money. It wouldn't be right to take advantage of the poor fellow. But the drunkard insisted. Finally, my friend took me aside and said the fool was going to lose the money anyway, so we may as well be the lucky ones. He suggested some sort of three-way coin flip. One of us was sure to win, and we'd split the money.

I do not remember the details, but, as with most cons, it appealed to my greed. I had only to put up the $40 in my pocket, and I couldn't possibly lose. We flipped, and, sure enough, my friend won. But no sooner had he taken the winnings and begun to split the money between us than the drunkard began screaming for a cop. My friend said the police would never believe we hadn't robbed the guy and took off running down an alley, yelling over his shoulder that he'd meet me back at the bus station. You guessed it: that was the last I saw of him. It wasn't much money, but the experience taught me a lesson I've never forgotten. If a deal seems too good to be true, you can bet it is.

Once home, I joined the US Air Force and headed back to Texas—this time to Lackland Air Force Base in San Antonio—for basic training. From there I was ordered to Biloxi, Mississippi to attend air traffic control school. It was not what I had hoped to do with my military time, but the training was useful eight years later, when I got my pilot's license. At the end of my air traffic controller training, I received orders for Japan. Although Japan was considered a choice assignment by most of the other guys in my class, I wasn't interested. I wanted to return to Texas, so I could be among people in the reptile business, to be part of the excitement. I headed directly to the Base Orderly Room and pleaded to have my orders changed. To my surprise, the Air Force went along with my request.

I spent the next few years at Randolph Air Force Base in San Antonio. Randolph was a training base for Air Force pilots. For brief periods, it had the busiest air traffic in the country—more even than Chicago's O'Hare Airport. I sat in front of two radar screens in a small trailer close to the runway called a Ground Control Approach (GCA) unit. On one screen I could see a blip showing an aircraft's azimuth position. The other scope showed the vertical position of the airplane as it flew down the glide slope toward touchdown. My job was to talk the aircraft down.

> "Turn right heading 272 degrees, you're 10 feet above the glide slope, adjust your rate of descent. Turn left heading 268 degrees, you're on the glide slope, resume normal rate of descent."

It was tedious work, but the lives of pilots depended on the GCA controllers. Radar accuracy was good, but not great, in those days. If a pilot were 50 feet left or right of what my screen showed as the runway center line, it was close enough. A quarter mile from touchdown, the pilot was expected to see the runway, or runway lights, and take over landing. Many pilots imagined we air traffic controllers were much more precise than we were, and we sometimes contributed to the myth. On pleasant summer nights we would talk a pilot down with the door to the GCA unit propped open. As the pilot neared touchdown, we would simply look out the door and continue giving azimuth and glide slope information by watching the aircraft landing lights. The moment we heard the sound of wheels touching the pavement, we'd announce "Touchdown now!" Pilots lavished us with praise for our incredible skill and accuracy.

While at Randolph, in 1961, I spent two weeks in Lackland Air Force Base hospital—the result of a life-threatening bite from a western diamondback rattlesnake. The base newspaper wanted to do a story about my interest in reptiles, and I had borrowed the snake from the San Antonio Zoo for an accompanying photo. I kept the snake with me leading up to the interview, quietly shuttling it between the barracks (where it wasn't allowed) and trunk of my car. One morning my friend, Larry Englehaupt, and I had been hunting rattlesnakes near base, when I became concerned about the trunk overheating. The sun was already blazing, and I wanted to check the animal's condition. I opened the trunk and spilled the snake out of its bag onto the ground. It was listless and apparently overheated. I pinned its head with my snake hook and picked it up in my right hand, thinking there was no reason to grip it tightly. Without warning, the snake regained its senses, whipped its body, and slipped loose. In the fraction of a second before I could drop it, it turned and bit me three times on the hand, between the thumb and forefinger.

I knew immediately that this was not a dry bite; I had been seriously envenomated, and excess venom spilled from the puncture wounds on my hand. I pulled a Cutter snakebite kit from my glove compartment. Snakebite kits were commonly used in those days and consisted of three rubber suction cups, a rubber constricting band, and a razor blade (snakebite kits are no longer recommended and generally do more harm than good). The idea was to tie the constricting band between the bite and the heart, just tightly enough to slow dispersion of the venom through the lymphatic system. The instructions called for making small incisions over the fang punctures, followed by an attempt to suck out the venom with the rubber cups. I instructed Larry on how to make the incisions, and, during the next hour or more, he made 16 X-shaped cuts, as the swelling progressed from my hand up my right arm.

I asked Larry to drive me into San Antonio, to the home of a friend named Jack Reid. I foolishly imagined Jack could treat the bite and put me up at his house until the danger passed. A knowledgeable amateur herpetologist, Jack took one look at the bite and insisted I receive medical attention. So he, Larry, and I high-tailed it toward nearby Brooks Army Medical Center. We were pulled over for speeding en route, but the patrolman saw my hand and led us directly to the emergency room. The physician on duty had no experience with snakebite and quickly arranged for me to be transferred to Lackland Air Force Base hospital. My hand was already very swollen, and Jack undoubtedly saved one of my fingers on the way to Lackland. I'd been wearing a ring given to me by my grandmother, and it had not occurred to me that, if left in place, it would constrict circulation and be impossible to remove. By the time we were in the ambulance, I couldn't get it off. Without hesitation Jack put my bloody finger in his mouth and, using his saliva as a lubricant, pulled the ring free.

The team of doctors at Lackland wanted to administer snakebite antivenom, but I was reluctant. I lied and told them that I had an allergy to the serum—something I couldn't possibly have known, since I had never taken antivenin for any of the four minor bites I experienced in the two years I'd worked for Jim Travis. In retrospect, my refusal was stupid. Antivenom is a custom-made fleet of antibodies that counteract the effects of venom and, at that time, it was made exclusively from horse blood. Many people experienced some degree of allergic reaction to horse antibodies, sometimes leading to anaphylactic shock. I was not concerned about shock, because I knew it could be controlled medically. But I mistakenly believed that antivenin, used improperly, could result in loss of a digit or even my hand. I remembered stories about one of Travis's employees losing his finger—the result, I was told, of a doctor administering antivenin directly into the bitten digit. The story was nonsense, but I was 18 years old and convinced I knew more than the doctors.

I left the physicians few choices. They decided to try cryotherapy, an experimental treatment advocated in the late 1950s and early '60s, but long since abandoned, since ice destroys tissue. The medical team packed my entire right arm in ice. After a few hours, I was delirious from the discomfort, and they removed it. The swelling moved steadily up my arm, across my neck and chest, and finally stopped, a few days later, halfway down my left arm. The pain was excruciating.

For the next two weeks, I received injections of antibiotics three times daily and kept the wound clean. The epidermis of my right hand split where the swelling exceeded the elasticity of the skin. Large blisters formed under the epidermis and filled with amber-colored lymphatic fluid that drained for days. The hand, and much of my right arm, turned purple from internal bleeding and black from necrosis. Even my left arm and inner thighs showed discoloration. It was not pretty. I survived, I suppose, because of my youth and physical fitness, but the doctors were convinced during the first few days that they were losing me.

Eventually I returned to base and took physical therapy daily for a couple of months in an attempt to regain full use of my hand. The therapy was successful, although, even today, that hand often aches and lacks the flexibility and circulation of the good hand. I was lucky that I didn't lose a finger, my hand, or my life. A venomous snake has never again bitten me. Sometimes it is possible to learn from your mistakes.

San Antonio was an exciting place to be stationed. Except during the Bay of Pigs invasion, when everyone was ordered to stay close to base, Larry and I drove each weekend to Lake Travis near Austin. There Bo Miller was building the Texas Serpentarium to winter his animals and keep his key people employed. Although Lake Travis was not a heavily traveled tourist destination, Bo had recently moved there from Houston and loved the area.

Bo was surrounded by odd and interesting people. Joe Wright, his sign painter, had been in the carnival business all his life, though, unlike most carnival artists, he could paint reptiles that really looked like reptiles. Joe made it clear that he considered himself an artist, and, from his stories, it seemed to me that he had been everywhere in the world. When I asked Bo about Joe's travels, he smiled and said that either Joe had indeed been everywhere or had read a hell of a lot of books. Bo's older brother, Mayburn, another remnant of the circus days, wore a large diamond stickpin that he claimed was valuable and told his wife that when he dropped dead, she should grab the diamond. It was her insurance policy. "Big Jim," one of Bo's sons, was reputed to be very successful with women, and another adopted son, also named Jim, but affectionately called Jim Bo, eventually took over the Soco Gardens zoo after his father died. Bo's wife, Clara, cooked huge meals, and everyone was invited to join in. I always felt as though I was part of the family. When my high school girlfriend, Virginia, and I married in a church in Austin, the Millers, the Travises, and many of their relatives attended.

My military assignment in Texas was not permanent, and I

expressed interest in going somewhere tropical like Vietnam, where open hostilities had not yet broken out. Instead, I was assigned to spend my last year of military duty in Greenland—as un-tropical a place as could be imagined. I've often wondered if, after my bite in Texas, the military brass sent me to Greenland to keep me as far away from venomous snakes as possible. When I left Texas I had the distinct impression that Bo intended to offer me a job upon my discharge from the Air Force. Sadly, that was never to be. During my year in Greenland—the same year President John Kennedy was assassinated—I learned that Bo had died of complications following an operation for colon cancer. The Texas Serpentarium died with him.

In many respects, my year at Thule Air Force Base in Greenland was pivotal. Bo was gone, and my plans to work for him dashed. I knew Jim Travis didn't have much to offer me professionally. There was little to do off-duty in Greenland, so I had plenty of time to read and ponder my future. And now that I'd been exposed to men with all kinds of backgrounds and with all kinds of (or lack of) religious beliefs, I struggled with my own religion. My parents were Lutheran. They believed in God, though when I went home on a two-week leave, halfway through my tour in Greenland, my father admitted that he, too, had doubts. As my dad grew older, however, he became very involved in the church, and I'm sure he came to regret insisting that I should always think for myself when I finally abandoned religion.

I talked and thought about religion a great deal in Greenland, and nothing about it made sense to me. I inched away from it with some trepidation—what if I were wrong? It was painful to give up a system I was raised with, and I first labeled myself an agnostic. Finally, after leaving the military, going into business, and continuing to search for something that made sense of life, I admitted to myself that I simply did not believe. Life without religion has not left me empty or bereft of basic human values. On the contrary, I have a cherished family and social circle and am fulfilled by the progression of science in human society. I continue to be fascinated by the near-ubiquity of religion, the power it wields in American culture, and its frequent clashes with science and societal change. No doubt religion had important value for our species during its early evolutionary history—possibly the glue that held tribes together—and we may be "hard wired" for it. But, as American philosopher and cognitive scientist Daniel Dennett points out, we're also "hard wired" to crave sugar, but we've outlived its usefulness.

CHAPTER 5
Reptiland – The Beginning

IN 1963, I ASKED my maternal grandfather, Clyde Foust, to loan me $10,000. My plan was to purchase a used house trailer and a towing vehicle with the money. I would convert the trailer into a traveling reptile exhibit and wander about the country to shopping malls, where I would charge shoppers admission to see my reptiles. My grandfather didn't refuse my request, but suggested he would be more enthusiastic if I used the loan to purchase property for a permanent reptile zoo. Since that was my ultimate goal anyway, I agreed and spent my year in Greenland planning and communicating with my parents, by letter, about a multitude of details.

Jim Travis had given up his zoo on US Route 15 and had no objections to my keeping the name Reptiland. My parents agreed to search the same highway for a suitable location and found four acres for sale just north of the small village of Allenwood. I received my discharge from the military in June 1964 and went immediately to look over the property. It was a farmer's field with approximately 600 feet of highway frontage. Five miles to the west is a tree-clad mountain range—part of the Appalachians—and, a half mile to the east, the beautiful West Branch of the Susquehanna River meanders south toward the Chesapeake Bay. Travelers heading south from the Southern Tier of New York State use Route 15, as do those northbound from Washington, D.C. and Harrisburg, Pennsylvania. I was delighted with my parent's choice. Within a few days of my return, we closed on the land.

I bought a 1953 Chevrolet pickup, purchased rough-sawn lumber from a nearby sawmill, and started to erect fences and an entrance building. Family friend Jim Opp built the plywood cages and hand-painted the road signs. Every weekend, and after work on weekdays, my father helped with electrical wiring, plumbing, and generally built anything I couldn't afford to purchase, which was just about everything. My mother prepared meals and brought them to the job site to keep us going. My 18-year-old brother Don worked with us every day. On July 11, 1964, we opened the doors to what could only be called a roadside zoo. Despite the support of friends and family, few people gave me much chance of success as I plunged into business with a lot of optimism and very little experience.

During construction of Reptiland we had been circumspect about the project, and few people knew what we were doing. On one of the many frantic days during construction, my father, brother, and I were applying corrugated metal to the roof of what would be the first Reptiland entrance building and gift shop. A car turned into the gravel parking lot, and a tall, lanky fellow about my age emerged. You can imagine my surprise when he gazed up at the three of us and asked, "What are you building, a zoo?" Yikes! How did he know?

That was my introduction to John Strawbridge. He told us he had worked for a small wild animal park in western Pennsylvania and recognized the similarity of construction (which meant built on-the-cheap). I admitted that we were building a reptile zoo, and John and I quickly struck up a friendship that has continued for half a century.

His father was an architect, and John grew up interested in art and animals in addition to design. He worked for me as a lecturer during the second year I was in business and did some design work for Reptiland. He was extremely influential in how my thinking about zoos evolved and in my taste for design. And it was John who first introduced me to the concept of Darwinian evolution, which helped me make sense of the natural world.

Sometime after we made Reptiland public—perhaps when road signs went up—a neighbor, who hated snakes, circulated a petition to keep us from opening. To my everlasting gratitude, the LaForme family, who lived next to Reptiland, came to our defense, and the petition died. Their son, Glenn, worked for us through high school, and they have been supportive neighbors throughout our history.

The early years of Reptiland were tough. During the first year, our biggest day resulted from a local newspaper article. We took in $300, and I thought we'd never again be able to top that. My first wife, Virginia, and I lived with my parents that winter, and, to supplement my income, I supervised a team of people taking the farm census for the federal government.

The next winter Virginia and I lived in an 8'x30' house trailer on the Reptiland property. She worked as receptionist for a local garment manufacturer, and I drove a tractor-trailer, delivering corn for a local hybrid seed company. The company owner, Milton Hoffman (who bore the predictable and true-to-character nickname "Seedy"), was notorious for not maintaining equipment; sending deliveries in overloaded trucks; and having no program to train new drivers. I received less than one hour of instruction from one of the older drivers and left the next morning before daylight with an illegally heavy load of corn. All went well until I reached the crest of a mountain near Laporte, Pennsylvania. In the morning darkness my rig began to gain speed on the downhill side, and I realized I had waited too long to downshift. I applied the air brakes, which worked briefly before the pedal dropped to the floor, and the rig accelerated rapidly. Forty, fifty, seventy miles per hour! I had no idea what curves lay ahead, but I knew it was too late to jump out of the cab. Remarkably, after free-falling for a couple miles, the truck gradually slowed as I reached the bottom and coasted to a stop along the side of the road. I sat there for a half hour as daylight broke, grateful to be alive and talking to myself in an effort to stop my foot from shaking. I don't think I have ever experienced that kind of fear, even while handling reptiles or flying airplanes.

My experience in the zoo business up to that point—working for Jim Travis and seeing what others, like Bo Miller and Arthur Jones, had done—persuaded me that Reptiland's success demanded certain indispensable components. There had to be big snakes, deadly snakes, and exciting shows (at the time, I was convinced that those shows had to include rattlesnake venom extractions, called milking). We built a fourteen-foot square and six-foot high wooden walled enclosure, surrounded by an elevated boardwalk. Visitors could stand on the boardwalk and look down into a "pit" crawling with rattlesnakes. The show was pretty hokey. We would leave our snake boots inside the pit and intentionally put a live rattlesnake in one. When a guide opened the door to enter the pit, he would begin to pull on the boots and, almost as an afterthought, stop to look at the audience as if to say, "Maybe I should check?" He would turn the boots upside down, gently shake them, and surprise—a rattlesnake would drop out of one boot. Invariably someone would exclaim, "Oh my God! How fortunate you had the presence of mind to do that!"

Our guides walked among the snakes while lecturing. At the end of each talk, the guide would pin a snake behind its head with a snake hook, pick it up in his or her hand, manipulate a fang into view, and gently apply pressure to a venom gland on the side of the snake's head. A drop of venom would ooze from the tip of the hollow hypodermic-like fang, and the guide would deftly flick the drop onto a finger. It was pure showbiz, although the lectures were factually accurate and otherwise delivered without a great deal of sensationalism. But one problem haunted me. The process resulted in death for the snakes.

To extract venom from a snake once a week would not be particularly detrimental, but we were doing it eight or ten times a day, seven days a week. There was no way in a pit of 50 to 100 snakes to ensure we weren't handling the same snake repeatedly. Walking among them day-in and day-out created stress and that, combined with over-handling and resultant mouth infections, killed the animals.

Within a few years, I knew I had to stop the show. I care about rattlesnakes and felt guilty that I was contributing to the decline of local timber rattlesnake populations. We instructed our guides to eliminate the handling and venom extractions. They continued to walk among the snakes, talk about them, and explain to our visitors why we no longer "milked" rattlers. I expected an angry outpouring and visitors demanding their money back, but, to my surprise, that didn't happen. Upon learning that handling killed the snakes, even ardent snake haters agreed with our new policy.

Unfortunately, snakes continued to die—possibly from our lecturers moving about among them or keeping so many snakes in close confines. We built a larger outdoor enclosure for native snakes with rock piles to provide hiding areas. The snakes continued to do poorly. Eventually we dispensed with the rattlesnake pit and converted it to a crocodilian exhibit. We learned that keeping fewer rattlesnakes in separate habitats was the key to keeping them healthy.

In those days, we seldom considered the threat of a lawsuit. If we engaged today in some of what we did then, we would be insane. During our first season, my brother Don worked as a lecturer. At that time we did not label each animal display, because we wanted the visitors to stay with the guide. If they could race ahead and read labels, they might leave without seeing a complete show and think they hadn't gotten their money's worth. We knew if they stayed with the lecturer they would enjoy the experience.

One day as Don was taking visitors on a guided tour, he noticed that he was having trouble keeping his audience with him. A number of people had clustered around something of interest across the compound. Don excused himself from his small group and walked over to invite the stragglers to join him. He quickly saw what had diverted the group's attention. The guillotine-style glass front of a cage had not closed completely. It was hung up, leaving a gap at the bottom. A venomous copperhead had escaped and was making its way along a rail in front of the cages. With his snake hook, Don scooped the snake back into the cage, without comment, and returned to his lecture. As he led his group around the compound he eventually arrived back at the copperhead exhibit. He explained that this small tan snake with hourglass chestnut bands was one of two venomous species native to our section of Pennsylvania.

A gentleman interrupted and asked incredulously, "Ya mean that thing is poisonous?" Don confirmed that it was venomous. "If I had known that I wouldn't have picked it up and had my photo taken with it!" he said.

When I heard Don's story, my knees wobbled. Copperheads, and even timber rattlesnakes, are docile by nature. I have seen foolhardy people handle both species without restraint and get away with it. Members of a few Pentecostal churches in Appalachia still handle them freely—testament, they believe, to their salvation. If they used western diamondbacks, a much more pugnacious species, it would be a real test! In spite of a copperhead's inoffensive nature they certainly can bite, and, although I am not aware of any fatalities, it is a very painful medical emergency.

In 1966, I received a letter from a young man named Jeffrey (I omit his last name for reasons that will soon be obvious) who lived in New York City. He wanted to work for me, and I hired him sight-unseen. When he arrived at the train station in Williamsport, I realized my mistake. He was carrying a bag that contained some sort of live reptile, and I asked him what it was. He had a speech impediment that made his response sound like "yellow monster." I didn't know what he meant and asked again, and again. On my third try, Jeffrey practically screamed out of desperation, and I finally figured out he was saying "Gila monster" (pronounced hee-la). Gila monsters are venomous lizards from the Southwestern U.S. The speech impediment was, of course, nothing Jeffrey had any control over; but I had hired him as a lecturer, and it wasn't a good fit.

I should have paid his ticket back to New York then and there, but I didn't have the heart, so Jeffrey spent the summer with us. He soon disclosed that his hero was Bill Haast, of the Miami Serpentarium. This should have been another red flag. Haast was well known for skillfully catching cobras with his bare hands, and Jeffrey, who did not impress me as being well-coordinated, soon pleaded to be allowed to free-hand my cobras. I refused. One day while he was cleaning the cage of a Cook's tree boa—an extremely irritable nonvenomous snake—a fellow employee with a warped sense of humor suggested Jeffrey practice free-handling with the boa. Jeffrey attempted to grab the snake directly behind its head, but his aim was off, and the boa sunk its long feeding teeth into his hand. Despite significant pain and bleeding, the incident didn't deter Jeffrey.

On his day off, he went rattlesnake hunting in the mountains near Laurelton, Pennsylvania and was bitten on his right hand by a timber rattlesnake—undoubtedly the result of some brash manipulation of the snake. His hand was badly swollen, and the doctor had put his arm in a sling to keep the hand elevated. Jeffrey thought he could continue doing rattlesnake venom extractions at Reptiland using his left hand. I steadfastly refused. On his next day off, he defiantly headed up the mountain toward Williamsport, reminding me that I might be able to tell him he couldn't handle rattlesnakes at work, but I could not tell him what to do in his free time. A few hours later

I got a call. Another rattlesnake had bitten Jeffrey, this time on his left hand. Could I meet him at the doctor's office? Jeffrey lasted only one season at Reptiland, never to return.

My parents, George Carlton and Charlotte Foust Peeling.

Boy Scouts played a role in my interest in reptiles in the 1950s.

My maternal grandfather, Clyde Foust.

I created a backyard zoo in my early teens at our family home in Clarkstown, PA, and this was my first brochure. Everyone called me "Bob" prior to my military service.

Part of the "thrilling show" at my backyard zoo in Clarkstown included an American alligator. Circa 1956.

My high school teacher, Evelyn Yeagle, encouraged me when few others did. She visited Reptiland in 2012.

Ross Allen was admired by every would-be herpetologist in the 1950s.

Jim Travis, who operated the first Reptiland "milking" a diamondback rattlesnake in the mid1950s.

Clara and Bo Miller at the New York Serpentarium, circa 1960. Photo by William Brown.

Bill Haast of Miami Serpentarium catching a king cobra.

Serving at Thule Air Force Base, Greenland, cemented my desire to build Reptiland (and my hatred of the cold). Circa 1963.

I discovered this picture of Arthur Jones hanging on the wall of animal dealer, Jesus Garcia's home in Colima, Mexico in 1971. Photo used with permission of arthurjonesexercise.com.

Like every snake "expert" of the day, I posed with the obligatory rattlesnake-in-hand in 1964. The knife was pure show biz.

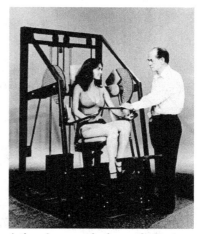

Arthur Jones with then-wife Terri on Nautilus exercise equipment. Circa 1985. Photo used with permission of arthurjonesexercise.com.

Holding a king cobra while my friend John Strawbridge (right) removed an eyecap, which the snake had failed to shed. Circa 1965.

My first anaconda, purchased from Tarpon Zoo in 1964, was not particularly large. Holding it with my brother Don (center) and employee Bill Ely (left), we posed to make it look impressive.

Rick and Mary Anne Hahn at the registration desk of the International Herpetolgical Symposium in 1988.

An early front sign at Reptiland. 1970's.

My co-worker, Dahle Bingamin, at the original Reptiland owned by Jim Travis. Circa 1959.

CHAPTER 6
On the Road

FOR A NUMBER OF YEARS we opened Reptiland on Memorial Day, closed after Labor Day, and housed the reptiles the rest of the year in a small building. I was embarrassed by our makeshift facilities and poured every dollar available into improvements. I wanted to be accepted in the zoo community, but it wasn't easy. I once called Roger Conant, then director of the Philadelphia Zoo and a well-respected herpetologist, to ask a question. He made no attempt to hide his disdain for "roadside zoos," and clearly lumped Reptiland among them. I thought the characterization unfair, since he had never visited the park nor had we ever met. I never forgot his cool reception. Many years later, his son Roger visited Reptiland, and I found the younger Conant to be warm and charming.

Gradually, I was able to borrow a little money from the bank and added a more substantial gift shop-entrance building to Reptiland. We had opened in 1964 with reptile cages covered only by a sun and rain shelter. Later I built a pole building similar to that used by local farmers. We still lacked a year-round reptile house with reliable temperature controls and had to move the collection to a small heated structure during the winter. We were able to keep animals remarkably healthy, but we needed better facilities.

I struggled financially. There was never enough money to get through the off-season, so in 1968 I began lecturing about reptiles to school children throughout the United States. An agent in North Hollywood, California, scheduled me for 460 lectures in schools in Nevada, California, Wyoming, Montana, Utah, and Idaho during the 1968-69 school season and another 230 lectures in Oklahoma that ran up until Christmas break in 1969.

I was on the road for extended periods, which presented challenges in keeping my reptiles alive and healthy. As ectotherms, these animals can't produce their own body heat–an aspect of their physiology misleadingly referred to as "cold-blooded." In the wild they regulate body temperature by crawling into and out of places heated by the sun; in captivity we have to supply the heat artificially. When I lectured in Montana, Wyoming, and Utah in the dead of winter, I filled hot water bottles in my motel room, packed them into the reptile travel boxes, drove to my first morning lecture, and refilled the bottles before heading to the next stop. It was a primitive, labor-intensive technique, but it worked.

Hydration was another challenge on the road. On any given evening, one could find an alligator, lizard, or snake soaking in my motel bathtub. In Salt Lake City, a python crawled out of the tub and across the floor while I was watching an evening television show. By the time I noticed, half the snake had disappeared into an air vent beneath a gas wall heater. I grabbed the snake's tail, which stopped it from going any farther, but the snake resisted being pulled backward. As I sat holding on to its tail, the snake's head occasionally emerged from the opening of the air vent, but I could not risk letting go in the hopes that it would continue crawling out and back into my room. If I turned it loose I feared the snake would disappear, and I'd never retrieve it.

What really concerned me was that, as I sat on the floor holding on to the snake, I could hear muffled voices in the next room. It gradually occurred to me that the gas heaters in each room sat back-to-back and shared a common air vent. What if the python ventured into the adjoining room? After a couple of frustrating hours, I hit upon an idea. I had a pocketknife and could just barely reach the curtain cord with my right hand, while holding onto the snake with my left. With considerable fumbling, I managed to cut the cord and tie it into a noose. The next time the python's head emerged, I slipped the noose around its neck and released my grip on its tail. By prodding the rear end and applying gentle pressure to the head, I guided the snake slowly forward, out of the vent, and back into my room.

My then-wife, Virginia, joined me for a brief period on the road. But touring for months at a time was not an ideal arrangement for a young married couple. The years had been rocky, and the marriage wasn't working for either of us.

When I finished my lecture tour in the spring of 1969 I headed east from California, across the Mojave Desert, through Arizona and New Mexico, and arrived in Austin, Texas for a brief visit with Jim Travis. While there, I bought an eight-foot male alligator. Travis and I built (more accurately, slapped together) a three-sided plywood platform to fit in the back of my station wagon. The "box" sat on top of the alligator and kept him restrained; the tailgate sealed the opening in the rear; and the back of the driver's seat created a barrier in front. I stacked my smaller reptile boxes and luggage on top of the alligator box and headed home.

The arrangement worked perfectly for the next day and a half. But passing through Knoxville, Tennessee, I was exceeding the speed limit on a wet road when a traffic light turned red. I hit the brakes, hydroplaned across the slick pavement, and collided with the rear of a woman's car ahead of me. Her car careered through the intersection, and everything in my car—reptile boxes, luggage, and the eight-foot alligator—slid forward, pinning me between the seat and the badly bent steering wheel. I couldn't extricate myself, but in the rearview mirror I could see people rushing to help me. The alligator had ambled toward the gap at the tailgate and was trying to escape through the open rear hatch. My would-be rescuers stopped dead in their tracks, mouths agape, as the alligator lumbered through the open window and onto the street. A nearby policeman was the only person willing to pry open the crumpled driver's door and help me out of the vehicle. I had sustained broken ribs, but was otherwise uninjured. The officer and I captured the alligator, lifted him back into the station wagon, and rigged a makeshift barrier at the rear.

Only then could we check on the condition of the woman in the other car. She was not seriously injured. I telephoned Bo Miller's widow, Clara, for help. Since Bo's death in 1963, she had remarried and was running an animal attraction in Pigeon Forge, about an hour out of Knoxville. Clara and her husband, Tom, came to my rescue, and we transferred the contents of my station wagon to Pigeon Forge for the night. The next day I rented a van, re-loaded everything, including the alligator, and headed for Pennsylvania.

Virginia and I divorced later that year. Before long, I met an attractive young woman named Dianne Mabb, who expanded my world view and my life. John Strawbridge introduced us and a short time later she visited Reptiland with her nephews. Dianne had grown up in western Massachusetts, attended college in Madison, New Jersey, and received her teaching degree from Columbia University in New York City. She read widely on a variety of subjects, seldom going anywhere without the latest copy of *The New Yorker* magazine. While at Columbia, she befriended an Israeli student and spent a few months on a kibbutz immediately following the 1967 Six Day War. Dianne is not Jewish, but she developed a keen interest in the culture and language and took Hebrew lessons for a number of years. In short, she brought a degree of culture to my life that I had never known.

I'm not sure when Dianne introduced me to sailing, but it may have been on our second date. Her father kept a small wooden Comet in the Susquehanna River, and she invited me to join her for a night sail. Trying my best to impress her, I wore leather soled shoes, a sports jacket, and dress pants—not ideal sailing attire. A mile or more from the dock, we could see a thunderstorm forming. She came about in an attempt to beat the storm, but, before we reached the dock, we found ourselves in the middle of a torrential downpour with lightning all around. Much to my embarrassment, Dianne dropped the sails, jumped overboard and pulled us ashore, trying to save my clothes, which by then were soaked anyway. We made our way to a nearby house whose owners invited us in out of the storm. I introduced myself as Clyde Peeling from Reptiland, Dianne's first hint that everything in my life revolved around the business. She was to learn over time that it would always be the case. I believe, though it sounds myopic, that to make it work a business requires total immersion—you have to eat, breathe, and sleep it. Of course, that kind of professional dedication can lead to shortfalls in other parts of your life. Fortunately, my family has stuck with me through them.

In the fall of 1969, I went back out on the lyceum circuit to about 200 schools throughout Oklahoma. Dianne remained in Pennsylvania, teaching English at my old high school in Muncy. She flew out to be with me on Thanksgiving break, and we drove down to Texas. In San Antonio, she received word her father was dying and immediately flew back home. I returned to Oklahoma and finished my lecture tour contract, which ended at the Christmas break.

During that time, Dianne and I wrote to each other almost daily. In one letter, she mentioned that she had begun taking flying lessons. My reaction was immediate–I had to learn to fly too. I couldn't let my girl friend become a pilot while I stayed grounded. I think that on the very day I received her letter, I visited the airport in Clinton, Oklahoma, and took my first of many flying lessons. As I traveled throughout the state, after my last program each day, I would rush to the nearest airport and take another lesson. Using different instructors in different towns is not the best way to learn to fly, since no two instructors teach in exactly the same way. Dianne, meanwhile, decided that flying wasn't for her and stopped taking lessons; sailing thrilled her more than flight. But I was hooked and have been a pilot since.

After returning to the east, in early 1970, I worked as a lecturer in Pennsylvania, New Jersey, and Long Island, pouring the proceeds back into Reptiland. I was able to see Dianne almost every weekend, and we married on March 21 of that year.

Among her other interests and skills, Dianne was a musician and church organist. Religion eventually became a bone of contention between us. When we met I had already given up the religion in which I had been raised, and I thought of myself as agnostic. While Dianne didn't accept the dogma of the church nor take the stories of the Bible as literal truth, she did feel there was a place for religion, and the music of the church spoke to her. Inasmuch as I preferred to avoid churches whenever possible, I seldom heard her play the pipe organ, nor truly appreciated her talent as a musician.

I've often joked that Reptiland's most successful breeding programs were the births of our three children. Dianne and I began a family soon after we married. Chad was born in 1971, Elliot came along three years later, and Whitney, our daughter, arrived in 1976. We raised the kids in a house on Reptiland property, and the zoo became their backyard. Our kids didn't think there was anything unusual about this. Like other families, we had pet dogs, cats and tropical fish in our house.

Occasionally zoo animals also shared our living space. About the time Whitney was born we raised a bobcat from a kitten in our home until it began to destroy furniture and its playful bites produced more than scratches. Everyone in the family still thought of it as a pet when we were forced to move the half-grown feline to an outdoor pen. But when Elliot opened the door one day to feed it, the cat pounced from behind a log, knocking the food out of his hand and tearing him up in the process.

I was home much of the time, but continued to lecture and run exhibits at sport shows in the off-season to make ends meet for the next twenty years, often traveling for extended periods.

CHAPTER 7
Seeing the World

REPTILAND'S GROWTH WAS SLOW and grueling. The zoo survived by sheer determination. I knew so little about business that I wasn't sure when we began making a profit. But at some point, perhaps without even realizing it, I was able to begin thinking about things other than our day-to-day survival.

Having been inspired years earlier by Arthur Jones, I had begun dabbling in film-making, and wanted desperately to travel. One winter day in 1971, my friend John Strawbridge and I loaded my Land Rover (a vehicle that suited my safari image better than it actually fulfilled my needs) with boxes of Bolex motion picture equipment and camping gear for a month-long speculative filming adventure. We drove southwest, passed into Mexico at Laredo, and continued down through Monterrey to our destination in Colima, on the western coast of Mexico. We were the only gringos in the entire state and were warmly welcomed by nearly everyone we met. A flamboyant Charro horseman and his beautiful wife invited us to set up our tent inside the walls of their hacienda just outside the city. From there we made day trips into the countryside to film.

It quickly became obvious that finding wildlife to film was not going to be easy. We decided our only hope would be to set up shots and asked where we might locate someone with animals. At first our guide, Manuel, misunderstood and took us to a taxidermist on a back street in Colima, whose creepy odorous studio was filled with dead armadillos and other stuffed wildlife. We narrowed our definition of "animals", explaining that we were looking for live, not dead ones, and Manuel finally introduced us to an old retired animal dealer named Jesus Garcia. When we entered Jesus's small house, he was wary of us until I noticed a photo of Arthur Jones hanging on his wall. Arthur, it turned out, had years earlier purchased animals from him and, despite being a non-believer, was godfather to one of Jesus's sons. Because I had met and admired Arthur, we were invited to join the family for dinner. The layout of the house did not make me especially hungry—a few feet to one side of the dining table was a coop of live chickens—but not wanting to offend our new friend, we accepted the invitation. The meal was good despite the occasional feather floating in the air and the animal hair John discovered at the bottom of his glass of milk.

Although Jesus was no longer active in the business of selling wild animals, he still had a few lying around. I bought a venomous beaded lizard, a relative of the Gila monster, a Mexican water moccasin, called a cantil—also venomous—and a few other specimens. We set up our shots in wilderness areas outside the city for filming.

Toward the end of our month in Colima, we camped near a banana plantation along the coast, not far from Manzanillo. Late one night we heard a vehicle approaching among the banana trees and headlights suddenly blazed through our mosquito netting. Four young men, quite loud and drunk, stumbled out of the car. This didn't look good. I tucked a smuggled pistol into my belt under my bush jacket and John and I went outside to meet them. The men insisted we join them for a drink and, hoping to avoid an altercation, we accepted. One of the men decided to go swimming. He sprinted headlong through thorny bushes that separated us from the beach, cutting himself up in the process. He stumbled back belligerent, deciding we were to blame for his cuts. Things looked like they might quickly go downhill, but his friends calmed him down and they camped there for the night by a fire. We went back to bed and woke early, broke camp while the men slept off their partying, and headed north. Although I occasionally used the film from the trip in lectures, the experience was really only valuable for its adventure.

Seeing that filmmaking was not a sustainable way to travel the world, I began to organize wildlife-viewing trips overseas, starting with the Amazon basin of Colombia, Peru, and Ecuador. Adventure travel did not provide a great deal of income for Reptiland, but it was in keeping with the zoo's developing mission to educate and entertain. People have always assumed that I travel internationally to bring back reptiles and amphibians for the zoo. In reality, the days of "bring 'em back alive" are long gone. Wherever possible, we obtain captive born animals; they're free of parasites, require fewer permits, and do not contribute to the depletion of wild populations. My trips were to places I had always wanted to go, and one way to finance the adventure was to have others share the experience. More than anything, the trips broadened my own view of the world, and of the wildlife and human cultures that inhabit it. Observing animals in the wild often translates into better captive husbandry and creation of more natural habitats. And being a group leader offered valuable lessons in improvisation and crisis management.

In 1989, on a group tour to Cuyabeno Wildlife Reserve in Ecuador's Oriente, we flew east over the Andes from the city of Quito to Lago Agrio. Once a small jungle village, Texaco pumping operations had turned it into a filthy, sweaty, sprawling oil town. All manner of businesses—dentists, doctors, restaurants, bars, hardware stores, and houses of ill repute—lined the muddy, trash-strewn streets. Our eclectic group of sixteen travelers ranged from a half dozen young Bucknell University students to a couple of retired elderly gentlemen, one in his late 70s. We retrieved our luggage from the corrugated steel shack that served as baggage claim and loaded into a bus—really a truck with wooden plank seats, open sides, and a flat roof that provided space for stowing baggage above and protected passengers from sun and rain below. We stopped briefly to purchase food at a market then took a road, following an oil pipeline, out of town through second growth rainforest.

A couple hours later we arrived at one of the many small tributaries that feed the Amazon basin. It had rained higher up in the Andes during the night, creating a much faster flow than is typical for Amazonia. Along with our bilingual guide we unloaded the baggage and awaited the Amerindians who had been contracted to take us into the jungle by dugout canoe. Time passed. No Indians or canoes. Obviously, there had been a screw-up, because an hour before sunset they still hadn't arrived. We noticed another Indian family—a man, his wife, and two small children—unloading bananas from their 45-foot dugout nearby. We hired them to take us downstream to our campsite before nightfall. A couple of locals with smaller canoes agreed to haul our baggage, and they left ahead of us since they were paddling and we would quickly catch up in the larger, outboard-powered dugout. Or so we thought.

The Indian family, our guide, and my group of sixteen piled into the giant canoe, which dropped the boat nearly to its gunnels. Water was within a few inches of coming into the dugout, and I questioned the guide about the wisdom of what we were doing. He discussed it with the Indian man, who reassured us: "no problem!" He cranked up the outboard motor and, as the canoe began to gather speed it rode higher in the water, exposing considerably more freeboard. I thought to myself, "He knows what he's doing—no problem."

Without warning we hit a submerged log at cruising speed, and the canoe flipped. I think we all had the impression that the stream was shallow. It wasn't, and everyone went under. I could hear the Indian woman screaming as she held her youngest child in her arms while her three-year-old daughter was swept downstream. Those of us nearest the inverted canoe held onto it, and others were swept to the opposite shore. One of the Bucknell students grabbed a tree root projecting into the water. As he did, he felt something bump his leg, reached down, and pulled the three-year-old to the surface. Another person rescued the elderly gentleman from our group, Mr. Betz, and pulled him close to the canoe where he could hang on.

Gradually we were able to maneuver the inverted canoe to shore, where everyone was accounted for—including the children. We watched helplessly as one student's Nikon camera case floated downstream. Other cameras, passports, and wallets were either swept away or soaked. But everyone was alive. The Indian man cut some long poles and, with our help, righted his canoe. Since the outboard motor had broken free and was now lost beneath the coffee-colored water, we poled the canoe to the opposite bank and retrieved the rest of our divided group. It was dark so we hiked the short distance back to where we had originally launched the canoe.

Next to a few nearby houses built on stilts, we encountered a woman with her children, preparing the evening meal. The woman was awaiting her husband's return from hunting, and was kind enough to let us spend the night. While we sat around her fire trying to dry out, a shotgun discharged nearby. Her husband returned shortly with a dead agouti, a large jungle rodent, which we shared for dinner. The students in my group stayed in one of the Indian houses—a great adventure for them, since a jaguar skin was draped on a side rail and a dried human hand hung from a rafter. The rest of us slept like cordwood, stacked side by side, in another house. It was a long and uncomfortable night, lying on bamboo slats with barely enough blankets to cover everyone simultaneously.

The next morning, we decided that the group would wait with our guide for the Indian boatmen we had expected the night before (surely they had gotten word that there was a mix-up). Mr. Betz, declared that he'd had all the adventure he could stand, and I accompanied him back to Lago Agrio. He was suffering from the dust and intense tropical heat, so I found a cool hotel lobby where he could spend the day. Meanwhile, I raced around town from one government office to another, filling out reports about our accident. Because we had lost some passports it was necessary to fill out police reports, which took the entire day and half a dozen bribes. Just before dark I returned to the hotel, gathered up Mr. Betz, and boarded a bus that took us over the Andes through the night. It was raining; the mountain road was treacherous with no guardrails, and the speeding driver either inattentive or insane. There was no way to sleep with chickens, pigs, and screaming children packed in the aisle, so we were both exhausted when we arrived back in Quito at about three in the morning. Dianne had remained behind in Quito and was surprised to find me knocking on her hotel door. I spent the balance of the week calling wives and parents for prescriptions for lost eyeglasses, asking for faxes of birth certificates, and finding additional money to replace what had been lost. The US Embassy staff was helpful and accepted faxed copies of birth certificates—not considered legal proof of citizenship at that time—to reissue passports. By the time the group returned to Quito a week later I had solved most of the problems, except replacing the lost cameras.

I returned to the Amazon many times in the 1980s and 90s, with clients and sometimes a family member in tow. Dianne has joined me on numerous South American trips but has never been drawn to the Amazon rainforest, probably because on her only trip into the jungle, she was uncomfortably pregnant with our son Elliot.

In 1983 I took our son Chad, then 12 years old, and a small group of travelers to the Amazon. We flew into Tabatinga, Brazil. From the air I could see tremendous deforestation on both sides of the mile-wide river that separates Brazil and Colombia. A decade earlier it had been virgin rainforest. In the airport we also saw changes brought about by illegal drug trafficking. Chad had gone into the restroom and locked the door behind him when a young soldier in oversized fatigues, and armed with an automatic weapon, demanded he unlock the door and submit to a body search. Local drug smugglers had begun using children as transport vessels, inserting cocaine-filled prophylactics into their rectums. The soldier insisted that Chad open the door, bend over, and spread his cheeks. I pleaded with Chad to unlock the door and let the soldier in, but he would have no part of it. In the end, the 12-year old's stubbornness outlasted the soldier's determination and we boarded a boat to cross the Amazon into Colombia without a cavity search.

Our daughter Whitney joined me one year in search of the elusive Black caiman– largest of the South American crocodilians. To find them we ventured down Ecuador's Rio Aguarico, enduring a 150 mile trip by dugout canoe to the Peruvian border. From there we motored up a tannic river to some black-water lagoons, where it is still possible to find large numbers of these endangered animals. Adult Black caimans can exceed 16 feet, but I have never seen one that long. We cruised slowly along the shoreline after dark, scanning the mangroves and reeds with flashlights for eye shine— the glow caused by tapetum, a mirror-like layer behind the retinas of crocodilians. When the light fixed on a pair of ruby eyes the boatman veered the dugout slowly toward the caiman and cut the outboard engine. Everyone remained perfectly silent as the Indians slowly maneuvered the canoe closer and closer. Once alongside the caiman, I made a grab for it behind the head.

Pound for pound, caimans are the toughest crocs to handle. When captured they often thrash and twist wildly. Holding on to a black caiman means enduring the especially rough scutes around the neck and back, each embedded with a small bone called an osteoderm. Imagine the letdown when I snatched a young thirty-inch caiman, and nothing happened. I had prepared Whitney and the others in the group to expect a lot of excitement, but the caiman lay almost limp in my grip. For a moment, I thought it may have been sick or injured;

then realized that its catatonic behavior was due to the shock of the capture. After everyone took some pictures I released the beautiful animal into the dark water. Back in familiar surroundings, it swam away, apparently no worse for wear.

People who have never visited lowland rainforest often have a mental picture—encouraged by movies—of giant anacondas lurking everywhere in the murky waters. In reality anacondas, and other large predators, are so stealthy, that they're seldom seen. I saw my first wild anaconda on an excursion with Elliot when we had taken a swim near the center of a blackwater lagoon (piranhas stay along the edges we were told). Our group clambered back into our dugout when we noticed violent commotion near the mangrove-tangled shoreline. The late afternoon light was fading rapidly and we encouraged our boatmen to get us closer to see what was causing the splashing. As we approached we could see a large anaconda—maybe thirteen feet long—constricting a five-foot black caiman within its powerful body coils. Naturally the caiman was fighting back. We sat next to the two struggling reptiles contemplating whether to catch the snake for photos. The Indians nixed that. They didn't like snakes. After everyone got a good look, I reached over and touched the anaconda. The startled constrictor released its grip on the caiman and both shot off in opposite directions beneath the water. Elliot and I headed back to camp for our evening meal.

Frustration and hiccups are par for the course when traveling in the developing world, but real danger is no fun at all. In 1990, I was back in Quito with a tour group that included my friend Bob Elion, a Williamsport attorney. We arrived late on a Thursday evening and met a mutual friend, Ted Hughes, who was teaching at an American school in the city. Bob and Ted shared an interest in mountain climbing and at the hotel bar Bob said he wanted to climb Pichincha, a volcano just outside Quito. Ted advised him of the best route to take, and Kim Brady, a young woman with us who was headed to the Galapagos instead of the Amazon, decided she would join Bob on the climb.

Early Friday morning I ate breakfast with Bob. Then he and Kim took off for the mountain while the rest of the group toured Quito with me. By dinner that evening, neither Bob nor Kim had returned, and I became mildly concerned. At midnight I went to bed, but awakened at three to discover that Bob had not returned to our room. I called Kim's room. No answer. I had the hotel staff unlock her room, where we discovered an unexpected stash of prescription medication and breathing equipment. Something was definitely wrong.

I couldn't sleep, so I rose early and met the group in the hotel lobby to explain the situation. I told them that they should continue into the Amazon with our guide. I would remain behind and catch up once I had located Bob and Kim. Reluctantly, they departed without me, and I contacted the US Embassy for advice. Embassy staff suggested I call the International Red Cross, and we soon arranged for a search party to scour the mountain. Meanwhile I went to the business office of the tour company I was using and began making telephone calls to find a helicopter that might be able to search from the air.

By noon a woman from the embassy joined me, and we took a taxi as far up Pichincha as the road went, got out, and surveyed the situation. Although I'm no mountain climber, from where we stood looking down into the caldera or up toward the summit, the climb didn't look too bad. The wind was howling at 14,000-feet, and it was obvious that our yells wouldn't be heard for any distance. As we stood there, the representative from the embassy gave me some chilling information. Someone had been murdering foreign couples on this mountain. My heart sank. I felt pretty sure Bob and Kim were dead, as Bob was a seasoned hiker and climber and fully capable of handling the terrain. As we took the taxi back down the switchback road to the city I scanned out the windows for any trace of clothing, or worse.

I contacted my family in Pennsylvania and had them call everyone I thought needed to know or could possibly offer assistance. I also tried to contact Ted Hughes, but he had gone off to climb Cotopaxi, another volcano some distance from Quito. I went to the police station in Quito, hoping the department might offer some assistance. The captain had been drinking and, even though I paid his bribe, provided no help.

Late the next afternoon, I finally located two US helicopters in Guayaquil on the coast. The operators agreed to send one up to Quito on Sunday morning to search Pichincha. I thought we were finally getting somewhere and fell into bed emotionally exhausted. My optimism was short lived.

I awakened Sunday morning to rain and poor visibility and knew the helicopter would not be coming. I went back to the tour company office and again telephoned Ted. He answered and agreed that, under the circumstances, Bob and Kim were probably dead. Even though he hadn't slept in 24 hours, he agreed to meet me at the tour office within an hour.

Then the phone rang. It was the International Red Cross. The voice on the other end said that Bob had been trapped on a narrow ledge with broken ribs since Friday afternoon but had managed to climb to the rim of the caldera during the night. He was on his way to the hospital. Kim, I was told, was still on the ledge with broken bones, but alive. I called her mother to give her the news. No sooner had I hung up than I got another call saying Kim was dead. I couldn't get reliable information and decided not to call her mother again until I was sure.

I met up with Ted and headed to the hospital. Bob arrived by ambulance at about 1:00 p.m. shivering under a blanket, his face scratched from climbing through brush during the night. He explained that while descending the caldera, he had fallen about 20 feet onto a narrow ledge, and was immobilized by pain. Kim, who had not previously revealed that she had a pacemaker and breathing problems, was too weak to retrace their steps for help. They weathered near-freezing temperatures by huddling together to share body heat Friday night. By late Saturday afternoon they realized a rescue might not reach them in time, and Bob mustered the strength to claw his way back up the caldera with one arm. The ascent took him all night. Bob said that Kim was alive on a precarious ledge when he left her Saturday afternoon and told us where to look. With a team of tough Ecuadorians, Ted headed for the mountain to rescue her.

By nine o'clock on Sunday evening—after three days and two nights on the mountain—Kim arrived at the hospital. I'd never touched anyone so cold who was still breathing. For hours I rubbed her arms and legs to try and transfer some body heat. Kim spent three days in the hospital before continuing her trip to the Galapagos. Bob was released a day earlier, but in no condition for rough travel with his ribs broken, so he rented a car and explored the market towns in the Andes. Meanwhile, Ted and I took a four-wheel drive vehicle over the mountains, dropping into the Amazon basin at Lago Agrio where we met my group.

In 45 years of trips, I have led dozens of groups to the Amazon, Galapagos, Indonesia, and East Africa. The vast majority of these adventures have come off without a hitch and they have enabled me to experience some of the last rugged environments on the planet. I have bellycrawled close to giant crocodiles in the windswept desolation of Lake Turkana in northern Kenya, a brutal region plagued by famine and malaria, which I contracted on one trip. I have witnessed the great migrations of grazing animals on the Serengeti plains and photographed big cats making kills. I have crouched on misty slopes among families of mountain gorillas, walked alongside giant monitor lizards on Komodo Island, and waded thigh-deep in bat guano to find reticulated pythons in a cave in Indonesia. Retracing Darwin's footsteps in the Galapagos Islands, I have swum with sea lions and visited ancient tortoises at their mud holes. I have been deep in the Amazon rainforest, traipsed through India on the backs of elephants, and explored blistering billabongs in northern Australia.

I still love to travel but, as I've matured, my appetite for roughing it has diminished. These days my trips are more comfortable, but I still lead groups to remote areas to see what remains of Earth's wild places.

CHAPTER 8
Reptiland Evolving

IN THE MID-1970S, John Strawbridge took a position as director of a museum adjacent to Hersheypark in Hershey, Pennsylvania. He called me one day to say that the old Hershey Zoo, which had closed following a 1972 flood, was in a state of decay. The site was becoming overgrown with weeds, the buildings were deteriorating, and HERCO, the entertainment arm of the Hershey complex, was debating whether the area should be used to expand the amusement park. John asked if I would join him in trying to convince the board of directors to let us build a new zoo on the grounds.

On the heels of the OPEC oil embargo Reptiland was cash strapped and we had borrowed money from Dianne's mother, Marie, just to make ends meet. I was happy for—and needed—the consulting work. John and I took our case to the HERCO board and they asked for a feasibility study. We returned a few months later with a plan and estimated cost. The board liked the concept, and I worked for the next couple of years, three days a week, as a consultant for Hersheypark's ZooAmerica, which would specialize in North American wildlife.

Being gone nearly half the week meant that someone else had to take charge of animal care at Reptiland. Our only full-time employee, Jeff Cook, a 19-year old reptile enthusiast from Toledo, Ohio, was the right person at the right time. Jeff took care of the animal collection, fixed things, chopped firewood, and generally kept the place operating while I was in Hershey. He worked at Reptiland for four years during some very lean times and later returned to Toledo to work in the aquarium at the Toledo Zoo. From there he went to Alabama and became Assistant Director of the Birmingham Zoo. With a wealth of zoo experience behind him, Jeff returned to Reptiland in 2005 to head up our animal department. He has been a friend and important part of the institution for more than 35 years.

John Strawbridge and I designed ZooAmerica as a series of North American biomes—the great Western plains, the frozen North, the Eastern woodlands, and the Florida Everglades. Part of the building devoted to the Everglades would include a short film. We persuaded the Goodyear Tire & Rubber Company to sponsor the film, and they arranged for us to use one of their blimps, the Mayflower, to obtain aerial shots. The Hershey job also paid me enough that I could buy the airplane I'd always wanted—and that would later prove invaluable to Reptiland. I loaded my film gear into my tiny Cherokee 140 and flew to Homestead, Florida. There I met up with Peter B. Kaplan, an accomplished still photographer who I believed would be a valuable assistant on the film shoot.

During the following ten days, Peter and I shot 10,000 feet of wildlife footage, which I eventually edited into a fast-paced, four-minute film for ZooAmerica. I am probably one of a small handful of private pilots who have logged time in a Goodyear blimp.

While in South Florida, Peter and I visited Bill Haast at his Miami Serpentarium. Haast was famous for having survived more than a hundred venomous snakebites during his daily venom extractions. Over the years, he had injected himself with small quantities of cobra venom to gradually build up antibodies that gave him some immunity to the venom of elapids, the family of snakes that includes cobras and mambas. Haast appeared often on *The Mike Douglas*

Show, a popular national TV program, extracting venom from adult king cobras for the viewing audience.

Haast had always kept himself lean and fit. He believed the adage of eating less and living longer, and it seemed to work—he was 100 years old when he finally died of natural causes in 2011.

I expected a warm reception from Haast when Peter and I visited. I'd met him a few years earlier, and he spent several hours graciously showing me the Serpentarium's manicured grounds and well-cared-for animals. On this trip, however, he was somewhat aloof. I later learned that the reception was not uncommon, depending on Haast's mood on any given day.

At the time, Haast had a large Nile crocodile named Cookie, which he had purchased from Arthur Jones. It was one of a group of crocodiles Arthur had captured in the Caprivi Strip (a wetland now part of Namibia). Cookie lived in a pool surrounded by a low wall, and I questioned the safety of the situation. The staff at the Serpentarium joked that Cookie had more than once crawled over the wall during the night, and they found him prowling the grounds in the morning. Not long after my visit, disaster struck. A visitor had placed his young son on the wall of the enclosure and encouraged the child to throw sea grapes at the croc to make it move. The child fell into the pool and was killed instantly by the crocodile. Haast, understandably distraught over the accident, decided to kill the crocodile. The death of the child was a tragedy, of course, but there was something deeply unsettling to me about the human response to kill a predatory animal as some kind of revenge or symbolic gesture.

The ZooAmerica project was stressful and briefly strained my friendship with John Strawbridge, but it also provided a creative outlet and an opportunity for the two of us to experiment with new philosophies in zoo design. Instead of a patchy menagerie of animals from all over the world, ZooAmerica was specialized. While working at ZooAmerica, I was also reinventing Reptiland in my mind. It was evolving from a roadside zoo into an educational institution. I wanted visitors to leave with a better understanding of the natural world and an appreciation for reptiles in particular.

I visited other zoological parks and observed what I thought were strengths and shortcomings. I noticed that large zoos often invested heavily in animals that interested the director. If the person in charge came up through the ranks as a bird keeper, resources were directed to the bird department, often at the expense of mammals or reptiles. It dawned on me that specialization might be a strength for Reptiland, rather than a weakness. We already had a well-defined niche, and by focusing on reptiles and amphibians, I thought, we might succeed in displaying them as well or better than major zoological institutions.

Animal care was improving too. Exciting things were being done in herpetoculture—the care of reptiles and amphibians in captivity—but innovators were scattered around the world without a forum to exchange ideas. While at zoo management school in Wheeling, West Virginia Rick Hahn and I talked into the night about how great it would be to bring all of these people together—hobbyists, zoo professionals, and academics—to share what each had learned about the nitty gritty of reptile care. Not long afterward we held the first symposium on reptile husbandry and breeding in Frederick, Maryland. I participated in the first two symposia, but Rick carried the torch for many years; the organization became the International Herpetological Symposium (IHS) and was a major catalyst in the expansion of knowledge and captive breeding of reptiles and amphibians.

Things were changing in zoos generally in the mid 1970s and inspiring work was being done at a few notable institutions. The

Sonora Desert Museum in Tucson, Arizona had pioneered the creation of naturalistic displays for native animals in the early 1950s. A few years later, Walt Disney opened Disneyland in Anaheim, California. Though not a zoo, Disneyland demonstrated innovative new possibilities that could be applied to animal exhibits. Its attention to detail—the artificial rocks, the trees and complex scenery—inspired those of us in zoos to create live-animal exhibits that more closely resembled the wild. Naturalistic exhibits presented animals in context and seemed to inspire a more respectful attitude from visitors than seeing specimens in barren cages.

Closer to Reptiland was the Bronx Zoo in New York. Its director, William Conway, had emerged as an impressive spokesman and philosopher about what zoos could, and should, be. I became friends with John Behler, the Bronx Zoo's then assistant Curator of Herpetology, forging an important personal relationship that lasted more than 30 years. About this time I decided to join what was then known as the American Association of Zoological Parks and Aquariums.

The AAZPA has since undergone a couple of name changes and is now the Association of Zoos and Aquariums, or AZA. Joining the organization helped crystallize my thinking about zoo philosophy, and about what Reptiland should become. John Behler would eventually push me years later to undergo the rigorous inspections needed for formal accreditation of Reptiland. This meant bringing our safety protocols, animal records, and keeper training in line with practices at the best institutions in the country. What I didn't realize then was that it was not just small zoos like Reptiland struggling to reinvent themselves in that era. The Bronx, San Diego, and St. Louis zoos were all looking for ways to break the old menagerie mold and be something better.

By the spring of 1985 we had prepared for our first accreditation inspection and Reptiland had never looked better. At 9:25 PM on May 31 everything changed.

Although rare in the east, conditions had been ripe all day for tornados. Unbeknown to us, more than 20 had already touched down in western Pennsylvania and had caused major destruction— toppling more than 85,000 trees in one state forest alone. We were next. The sky to the west of Reptiland had been ominously dark even before sundown. I was talking on the telephone when I heard a roar. I ran from my office into the gift shop. Outside, all manner of debris—tree limbs, paper, leaves, boards—was flying horizontally across the zoo parking lot. My family joined me and we foolishly stood in front of large plate glass windows—that somehow escaped the flying missiles—watching in amazement. The wind blew, we would later learn, at over 200 miles per hour—an F4 tornado. I ran to the back door to see what was happening inside the zoo and could see nothing through the wall of blowing water. The building trembled and groaned, but it held together. Twenty minutes after the storm hit us, it moved on.

It was dark outside. The entire area had lost electricity. The air was eerily quiet, as if the normal sounds of spring had been swept away. Eventually the faint sounds of sirens of emergency vehicles could be heard in the distance. We located flashlights and ventured into the zoo. Electrical power lines lay strewn about on the ground. Our outdoor pens were badly damaged or completely missing, but the reptile house was still intact. Trees on both ends of it had been uprooted and fallen away from the building—rather than into it. No reptiles had escaped. That was a relief. Being careful to avoid power lines I followed the raucous voices of our two macaws. A tenth of a mile away, the disheveled birds were perched next to their crumpled pen which had gone airborne during the storm. In the end only a couple of fallow deer were missing which we eventually recaptured. We found one dead peafowl—the only animal fatality.

Our family was shaken but uninjured. Not all neighbors were so lucky. A quarter mile north a woman was killed in a local campground and a trailer home crushed a small child just east of the zoo. The tornado had cut through the valley ravaging everything in its path.

My brother Don arrived with a chain saw and generator within a couple hours of the storm, having heard about it on the radio. We plugged in freezers and waited for dawn. The next morning we surveyed the damage. Trees were down. Fences had been flattened. Shingles had blown off roof tops. Reptiland was a mess. As the news spread friends arrived to help clean up. Some came with hammers and began rebuilding fences. Amish farmers, a county judge, and people we didn't know appeared out of nowhere. Remarkably, a week after the storm hit Reptiland, reopened for business.

We were back in business but very rough around the edges. Accreditation had to be put on hold as we recovered. AZA granted us a year's extension on our accreditation inspection and Reptiland finally became an accredited institution in 1986. Like all accredited zoos and aquariums we undergo the review process every five years. The process is expensive and exhaustive, and we're one of a few small privately owned zoos to have made the effort. Businesses and institutions evolve in much the same way species do. In many cases an adaptation that lends an advantage for one aspect of survival becomes a fortuitous pre-adaptation for something entirely different. Joining AZA and becoming accredited marked a critical and transformative adaptation for Reptiland. It pulled us into the era of modern zoological institutions and prepared us for the next stages in our evolution.

Besides becoming an accredited zoo, Reptiland in the mid-1980s was becoming a family business. By the time my son Chad was fourteen he had already developed an interest in reptiles, and we allowed him to help the keepers with husbandry duties. He was, of course, not permitted to handle venomous snakes at that age (but with teenagers, rules are not always followed). One day an experienced keeper named Clair Thompson was lecturing to a group of visitors under an open-air shelter when Chad appeared from behind the reptile house and bolted past the audience, an expression of concern on his face and holding his finger. Clair excused himself and ran after Chad, asking what had happened. Chad replied that he'd been bitten by a venomous snake. One of our visitors, visibly concerned, asked about our procedure in such an emergency. Clair, in typical fashion, replied, "Shit and git."

Chad had moved a purple-spotted viper, a venomous Asian species, on the end of a snake hook and gotten his hand too close. The snake struck out and sank one fang into his right index finger. I submerged the finger in a glass of cold water to slow swelling and contemplated the situation. The snake was a juvenile and I knew it probably could not have produced life-threatening symptoms, but there are occasional medical anomalies and people have died from what seemed like minor bites. This was, after all, my kid.

We called Geisinger Medical Center in Danville for transport and met a Life Flight helicopter at the landing strip where we kept our airplane about a mile and a half north of Reptiland. There was no room in the helicopter for me so I jumped in the Cherokee and flew to Danville Airport, where I hitched a ride to the hospital. Chad was already in a room in the intensive care unit when I arrived. The injury certainly did not justify a stay in the ICU, but the extra attention he received there was comforting.

The medical staff had taken his finger out of the cold water and the area was swelling. The skin of the hand was already tight and he was in real pain. Despite the swelling, doctors applied warm compresses to the hand to increase blood flow and disperse the venom away from the finger, a measure I thought wise. A surgeon was called in and his immediate suggestion was to perform a fasciotomy, which involved filleting the finger with deep cuts to relieve pressure building in the enclosed muscle compartments. Even then, the consensus among doctors with experience treating snakebites was that fasciotomy was generally inappropriate. I objected and said that the bite did not appear to justify such a traumatic procedure. The surgeon haughtily replied that if it was necessary, it was necessary, and he'd have to do it. I held my tongue but was determined I would not permit it. Fortunately, the surgeon never returned. Perhaps he consulted the literature and confirmed my objections. Chad did not require snakebite antivenom and suffered no lasting physical effects from the bite. He did gain a healthy respect for venomous snakes and we improved safety procedures at Reptiland.

CHAPTER 9
The Second Generation

IN 1990, AFTER MORE THAN 25 years in business, Reptiland faced the first genuine challenge to its existence since the early hand-to-mouth days. A politically-connected corporation with a dodgy environmental track record tried to build an industrial hazardous waste incinerator on a 700-acre property adjacent to Reptiland. It took some time, and the determined digging of a reporter at the *Williamsport Sun-Gazette*, to establish that an incinerator was being planned for the site—originally, the community had been told it was to be a soup factory. Some soup! With the help of like-minded citizens in the area, we revived a dormant activist group called Organizations United for the Environment (OUE). I helped start OUE in the mid-1970s to fight a multi-county landfill. We were unsuccessful then, and feared the incinerator might also be unstoppable. But, after four years of near-constant legal battles, a peaceful sit-in at the Department of Environmental Resources building in Harrisburg during which some friends and I were arrested, and countless community meetings (including one where we were joined by actor and activist Ed Begley, Jr.), we prevailed. The project was dead in the water and the 700-acre property was purchased by the county.

The incinerator fight marked a difficult time for me personally. The same year the fight began my father died of a heart attack. Losing him, combined with the constant stress of holding a fractious community organization together and battling a corporate behemoth, took a toll. But it also marked a turning point for Reptiland. With my attention almost completely diverted to the environmental fight, day-to-day operations fell to others. Chad was in college and worked weekends, holidays, and between classes, managing the animal care and interpretation staff. I had recently hired a capable young woman named Chris Bergesen as our first full-time gift shop staff member and she quickly absorbed a great deal of responsibility. Elliot became more involved over the next couple of years and, by the time the incinerator fight was over, Reptiland had lurched into the second generation, poised to support three families.

Chad completed a four-year degree in Zoo Management, a customized major combining biology and business curricula at Susquehanna University. He joined the staff full-time in 1993 and has spearheaded zoological operations since. He and Chris eventually fell in love and married. Chris managed the Reptiland gift shop for twenty-five years, transforming it into a world-class zoo store. She also harangued until I finally agreed to build a butterfly exhibit, followed two years later by an outdoor display of animatronic dinosaur models. Both have been hugely successful additions to Reptiland. While raising two sons, Pierce and Evan, Chris also managed our marketing department, came up with clever titles for traveling exhibitions, and booked me on national television shows.

Elliot always had an interest in how things are built. He learned computer-aided design (CAD) in high school and studied construction and design in college. Like my father, he always seems to know intuitively how to build things, and how to build them just right. He entered the business full-time in 1995 and began to rebuild what had been slapped together over the previous years. Elliot created, and manages our design and fabrication department and has had an indelible influence on every project we've done.

Each of our children is hard working and has acquired talents far beyond my own. Our daughter Whitney was always a happy, fun-loving child. Although she worked at Reptiland as a teenager sweeping the parking lot, cleaning restrooms, and clerking in the gift shop, she never developed a love for the business. After high school she attended Columbia University in New York City and went directly from there to work in the publicity department for the publishing firm Houghton Mifflin. She subsequently worked for W. W. Norton and PublicAffairs, a company specializing in books with a political bent. Today, she is a freelance publicist and works for a variety of authors and publishing houses.

Whitney seldom misses an opportunity to mention that she grew up in a reptile zoo (her first boss in publishing told her later that the family zoo on her resume was what landed her the job). Through the years, she has worked with interesting and high-profile writers from many fields, and she has brought Reptiland along for the ride. While an assistant publicist with Houghton Mifflin, Whitney introduced us to evolutionary biologist and author Richard Dawkins. Following a lecture at nearby Bucknell University, Dawkins visited Reptiland. He asked questions, offered opinions and shared lunch with Chad, Chris, and I before heading to the airport. It was a memorable experience with an exceptional thinker.

Family business is tough. Working with people you love and with whom you share life history brings all kinds of challenges—we often disagree, professionalism sometimes gives way to personal acrimony, and you can't leave your work problems at the office when you go home. But the coalescence of skills and energy brought by the second generation has grown Reptiland into an entirely different company, far beyond anything I would have achieved on my own.

Part of that growth—like many great ideas—was born of desperation. In 1996 we built a much larger indoor exhibit building to house the living collection and give us space to grow. It was, at the time, a huge investment and really more than we could afford. It became obvious that we needed additional income streams. In 1997, Chad returned from a trip to Maryland, where he had seen a lackluster temporary exhibit rented by a museum to boost attendance. We decided to investigate the idea of creating large-scale traveling exhibitions that feature live reptiles. Only one exhibition was filling that niche at the time and Elliot and Chad made a road trip to check it out at a museum in the Midwest. They returned convinced we could do it better. But breaking into the traveling exhibition business proved a challenge. At the time, we were scarcely making payroll. Where were we going to come up with hundreds of thousands of dollars to create and build an exhibition that took Reptiland on the road?

Our solution was to design the exhibit on paper and construct a couple of sample components while we tried to get a booking. Elliot created a detailed scale model of the entire exhibition, complete with graphics and plants. We photographed it, created a promotional brochure, and mailed it to museums throughout the United States. For months nothing happened. Then one day I received a telephone call from Libby Lewis at the Liberty Science Center in Jersey City, New Jersey, expressing interest in booking the reptile exhibition. Then she questioned the photo on the brochure, "Is that a model?" My heart sank. I was sure she would lose interest when I admitted that it was. But when I explained we were in the process of building, she was undeterred and wanted to visit our shop to observe the progress. Libby saw only two walls completed with habitats, but she must have been convinced we could pull it off. She called within two weeks, and we had the first of many bookings with traveling exhibitions.

Lecturing kept Reptiland afloat in the off-season and I performed thousands of educational programs at schools throughout the US. My first airplane, a Cherokee 140, allowed me to perform in the tri-state area and be home most nights. Circa 1976.

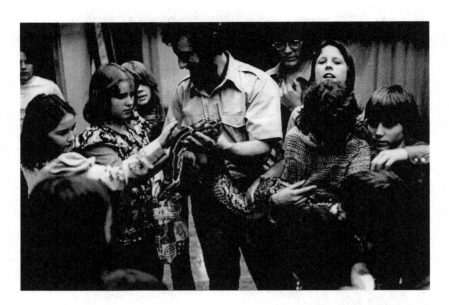

Interpreting reptiles has been a major focus at Reptiland and in off-site programs.

Adventure travel exposed me to many cultures and natural habitats. Top to bottom: tenting in Mexico while filming with John Strawbridge; my Land Rover provided impractical—if perfectly styled—transportation on North American trips; standing with an early tour group in front of a kapok tree in the Amazon rainforest; filming a wildlife documentary for Goodyear in the Everglades .

The Peeling family circa 1980. Clockwise from top: Clyde, Dianne, Whitney, Elliot, and Chad

Reptiland's rattlesnake pit exhibiting native reptiles, circa 1972.

Our first permanent reptile house and an adjacent outdoor tortoise exhibit. Circa 1972.

Chad Peeling atop an Aldabra tortoise, 1973.

A view of Reptiland's compound—spartan, but tidy. Circa 1970.

Reptiland's rattlesnake pit was converted into a seasonal exhibit for crocodilians when we realized it was impossible to keep snakes healthy in large groups. Circa 1980.

CHAPTER 10
On the Air

MY FIRST APPEARANCE ON a national television show was *To Tell the Truth* with Gary Moore in the early 1970s. I sat with two other Clyde Peeling "imposters" and answered questions for a celebrity panel that included Kitty Carlisle, Nipsey Russell, Bill Cullen, and Henry Morgan. The fact that they picked one of the other safari-clad gentlemen as the "real" Clyde Peeling didn't make me feel famous, but the experience was fun. It would be another 20 years before I did more national television. In the interim, I got an on-camera education courtesy of Arthur Jones.

In the early 1980s Dianne and I packed up the kids each winter and headed for Florida to visit her mother, who lived in Deland. These were exciting years for me, because the little village of Lake Helen, where Arthur Jones lived, is only a short distance from Deland. It gave me the chance to know Arthur well and led to some valuable experience in front of a camera.

I had tried to keep track of Arthur in the years after meeting him in 1960. I was in Austin in 1961 when he flew in for the grand opening of Bo Miller's Texas Serpentarium. Sometime later I heard that Arthur had been killed in a plane crash. But in 1968, I stopped at a roadside reptile zoo in New Braunfels, Texas, and asked the owner, who knew Arthur, if the rumor was true. He had heard the story, he said, but on a recent trip to purchase animals from Bill Chase, an animal dealer in Miami, he had discovered Arthur drinking coffee in Bill's back room. He claimed Arthur had spread the rumor to throw off the Internal Revenue Service. When I asked Arthur about the story years later, he responded, "Most of what they say about me never happened and they don't know about a lot that did."

While lecturing at a sports show in Minneapolis during the winter of 1973, I mentioned Arthur Jones with regard to crocodiles. Following my program a young man approached me to ask whether this was the same Arthur Jones who wrote articles for *Iron Man* magazine, a publication about weight training. I remembered that Arthur had kept weight lifting equipment in one room of his home in Slidell, and replied that I thought it was possible. The next day the fellow returned to the show with some articles for me. As I read them I knew it was Arthur. He wrote exactly like he talked, and from the articles, I learned he had started a company called Nautilus and was manufacturing exercise equipment in Lake Helen.

On the first trip with Dianne and the kids to Florida, I couldn't wait to search him out. I remember walking into the Nautilus headquarters and asking if he was in. "And who shall I say is here?" inquired a woman behind a desk. I explained that he wouldn't remember me, but to tell Arthur I had visited him in Slidell in 1960 with Jim Travis. With that, Arthur emerged, and I spent the entire day with him, and at least one day every trip to Florida for the next decade. He was one of the most innately intelligent people I've known. He had incredible energy and talked almost continuously, but was always interesting and had a wonderful storytelling patter. He could be, and often was, crude. People either loved him or found him disgusting. Women sometimes recoiled at his outlandish statements. "There are only three things of value," he loved to say, "younger women, faster airplanes, and bigger crocodiles."

Dianne could never appreciate my fascination with Arthur, but many years later, when he stayed overnight at our home as an old man, even she admitted he had an undeniable charm.

Our family enjoyed the things most families do when vacationing in Florida—visiting Disney World, Busch Gardens, Sea World, and exploring natural areas like Blue Springs by canoe. But at least once every visit, sometimes twice, I'd break away while Dianne and the kids spent the day at the beach and head for Lake Helen to spend the day with Arthur.

Arthur projected a tough exterior, and he was tough. He was not big, but he was lean and muscular, much stronger than he appeared because he generally wore loose-fitting, long-sleeve shirts, probably to cover some tattoos. He could be ruthless, but also surprisingly kind. On one of my visits, he told me to get into his car—Arthur never asked—and we drove to a nearby apartment building where a former animal dealer, Ralph Demure, was slowly dying of emphysema. Because Ralph had trusted Arthur years before and extended credit when few others would, Arthur paid his rent, bought his groceries, and checked in on him periodically. Ralph was attached to an oxygen tank, and we sat and talked at his kitchen table. Like Mark Twain, who famously never let schooling get in the way of his education, Ralph claimed to be proud to have had only a high school education. He looked at me and asked if I had gone to college. I responded that I had not. "Neither did Arthur or me," said Ralph with a smile and some satisfaction. "We went to the 'school of H.N.'"

I thought about that for a second, assumed he was referring to hard knocks, and asked if he didn't mean the "school of H.K.?" Arthur quipped that apparently neither of them had learned much.

In the mid-1970s, Arthur used some of his Nautilus fortune to build a giant television complex with seven sound stages in Lake

Helen—at the time he was Sony's largest customer. He foresaw the fragmentation of television (a decade too early as it turned out) and was producing programs about exercise, cooking and all manner of other subjects. Arthur invited me to "strap my airplane on my ass" and fly down to tape some programs about reptiles. We taped a series of highly-produced episodes, and he invested significantly in the project. Although nothing came of the programs we made, the opportunity provided me hours of experience in front of television cameras, which would prove valuable years later when I began appearing on late-night talk shows. On one of the taping trips, I stayed with Arthur at his home in Lake Helen. He had just fallen madly in love with Terri, a stunning, 17-year-old beauty contestant. Arthur was by then a multi-millionaire in his fifties.

Had I noticed Terri, he wanted to know? Yes, I wasn't blind. He pulled me aside and asked if I knew anything about human physiology. I felt something coming, and tried to avoid a trap. I said that I knew very little about the subject. Did I know why a man's testicles sometimes hang suspended and at other times recede into the body cavity? I replied I was pretty sure it had to do with temperature control. Did I believe it possible for a man's testicles to touch the ground while standing in an upright position with his legs slightly spread? I raised an eyebrow in doubt. With a symbolic swipe of his hand suggesting he had a knife at the appropriate location he said, "Of course they'd be severed right there. That's what'll happen to you if you even think about it!"

I began a run of national television appearances in the early 1990s when my daughter-in-law Chris Bergesen booked appearances for me on a number of major shows including *The Jon Stewart Show*, ABC's *Regis and Kathie Lee* and NBC's *Late Night with Conan O'Brien*. Those appearances led to additional shows—more than a dozen with Conan and several on NBC's *The Tonight Show with Jay Leno.*

On one of the *Tonight Show* appearances the obligatory young actress on the show (producers always felt the need to pair attractive actresses with my appearances so they could react to the animals) was former model Jenny McCarthy. Leno's writers had put together a short skit to open the show. Jay came into my dressing room and asked if I had found his gift. My line was, "Yes. The flowers are beautiful." "Flowers?" asked Jay, with a bewildered look. The next shot cut to Jenny in her dressing room unwrapping the gift intended for me; a box of live white mice. She grabbed one by its tail, dangled it above her open mouth as though she intended to eat it, while smacking her lips and saying how much she loved mice. It was a good gag. Although I did not do a particularly convincing acting job, Jenny McCarthy made it work.

For that appearance I had rented animals from Mark Biancaniello, who was working at the time as manager of Michael Jackson's Neverland Ranch, in California. Mark arrived with a 150-pound alligator snapping turtle from Neverland, and we wheeled the turtle into the studio in a thick plywood box for rehearsal. I had always believed that alligator snappers had proportionally less jaw strength than the common snapping turtles found in Pennsylvania. I had never been cavalier about getting my hand close to an alligator snapper's gaping jaws, but thought tales of snapping broomsticks were overstated. As Mark and I struggled to lift the turtle out of its box, however, the snapper clamped onto the top rim with such force it crunched the three-quarter-inch plywood. I have no doubt now that an alligator snapper that size could crush a hand, if not sever it. In the same show we used Michael Jackson's anaconda, the largest specimen of this South American species I have ever seen. The snake was easily 17 feet long and 300 pounds. A lot of reptile books mention 20-foot anacondas as though they are common, but giant snakes tend to shrink when a tape measure is stretched along their length. Believe me, a 17-foot anaconda is a big snake.

This one was not tame, nor was it accustomed to being handled.

We grabbed the snake just behind the head, and seven people took sections of its incredible bulk as we pulled it from its box. Excited anacondas often emit foul-smelling musk from either side of the tail and this snake was definitely excited. It writhed, fought, and musked profusely to the disgust of Jenny McCarthy, who was holding the back end.

Having spent my career educating audiences about reptiles and other animals, I tended to try to cram as much information as possible into the brief seven minutes I was given on-air. But late night TV is not a *NOVA* special; you're there for levity. In time I came to understand that and appreciate the appearances on their own terms. No matter whether the animals did what we expected or not, they are spectacular to watch and usually made the segments work. Assembling animals for television appearances in New York or Los Angles is no small task. Late night shows usually want "wow" animals that are big or dangerous or will "do something." When we receive a call asking whether we can do a show, we seldom have more than a week, and usually less time, to locate suitable animals. Once we track down the animals—ours or someone else's—we have to obtain permits. This is usually a nail-biting affair, since most permitting agencies are not noted for quick turnaround times. More than once I've headed toward New York City with a load of animals, without permits in-hand and learned by telephone just before crossing into the city that the permits had arrived.

Each state has its own wildlife regulations as do many large cities. At the national level, the U.S. Fish and Wildlife Service (USFWS), Department of Agriculture, and Centers for Disease Control (CDC) write and implement most of the federal regulations relating to terrestrial animals. These agencies are staffed by many good, hardworking people and regulations are typically written with good intentions. But navigating a labyrinth of well-intentioned regulations creates tremendous inefficiency. At the time of this writing, a permit to move an injurious species across state lines or an endangered species from the US to Canada takes three months or longer. If the purpose of the move is for an educational exhibition or television show, it may mean cancelling. If it's for captive breeding, the move may come too late for the species' reproductive season, and an opportunity to breed a rare species is lost.

A seven minute television appearance with live animals may—depending on the species—require four separate city, state, and federal permits as well as health certificates to enter New York City.

Once at the studio, the animals are moved by elevator to the appropriate floor where the show is produced. For one show we borrowed a five-foot nurse shark from Jenkinson's Aquarium in Point Pleasant, New Jersey. The aquarium staff transported the shark in a large tank complete with aeration equipment. We had to use a forklift to get the tank out of the van and on and off the elevator—all this for a few minutes of show time.

On another show, two young people from a Florida zoo drove up to New York with a number of animals including a llama. It was in the dead of winter, and they spread a tarp onto their motel floor so the animals could be brought in out of the cold. The next morning as they began reloading the animals, the llama suddenly bolted and ran into the morning rush hour traffic on the nearby interstate highway with my two friends racing frantically after it. Eventually they rescued the llama. When they met me at the studio later in the day, neither of them mentioned the incident, fearful that word might reach their director back in Florida.

CHAPTER 11
Reptiland Branching Out

I HAD ALWAYS DREAMED of developing multiple locations for Reptiland, much as Bo Miller had done with his zoos. In 1991 we bought a defunct facility in Catskill, New York and opened a smaller version of Reptiland near the once famous Catskill Game Farm. The heyday of the Catskills was gone, but I believed the scenic beauty of the area had enduring appeal. We kept the facility open for seven seasons, bringing the animals back to Pennsylvania each fall. But operating an entire business at that distance—staffing, advertising, property maintenance, cash control—was difficult, and traffic in the area was waning. We sold the Catskill property in 1998 just as we began building traveling museum exhibitions.

For a prestigious museum to allow an outside firm to bring living, sometimes dangerous, animals into their galleries takes real trust. Our AZA accreditation reassures host institutions that we abide by professional standards of animal care and safety, but it has taken years to build relationships in the industry. Traveling exhibitions have enabled us to reach large audiences in metropolitan areas and extend the reach of our educational mission. They have also helped pay the bills.

Our first traveling exhibition, *Reptiles: the Beautiful and the Deadly*, premiered in 1999 and continues to tour, having undergone several rejuvenations. Our follow-up project, *Frogs–A Chorus of Colors*, features live frogs from around the world. This exhibition has proven so popular that we built a second unit to tour simultaneously. John Behler and his wife Debbie asked if they could use the title of the exhibition for a chapter in their book about amphibians, and we encouraged them to use it as the book title instead. They published the book as a companion to the exhibition. It was to be their last book together, as John died prematurely of heart disease in February 2006.

We followed *Frogs* with *The Scoop on Poop*, an exhibition focused on the science of what animals leave behind. And a few years later we opened *Geckos–Tails to Toepads*, a highly interactive look at one of the most successful groups of lizards. Success with traveling exhibitions led to the creation of an exhibit fabrication department and changed the trajectory of our business. In addition to traveling exhibitions, our design and fabrication team creates custom exhibits for installations at other museums and zoos. Our work can be seen in dozens of institutions nation-wide and abroad—and, of course, at Reptiland.

There is significant crossover among staff in any small business, but Chad and I generally come up with exhibit themes and write interpretive materials. Elliot designs the physical components, including the intricate details of packing for shipment and rapid re-assembly. Our animal care team maintains the living collection and provides daily onsite care for traveling exhibitions at host facilities; our fabrication crew builds components and oversees setups/teardowns; our graphics and marketing team produce multi-media content and keep the exhibits booked. It's a team effort.

Traveling with live animals requires extraordinary logistics. Our staff technicians meet the trucks carrying physical components and set up an exhibition in a museum gallery several days before we move animals. After habitat temperatures are stabilized and filtration systems activated, we transport the animals to the site packed in insulated coolers with ventilation and heat or cool packs as needed. The goal is to move quickly and minimize stress on the animals—it sometimes feels like we're transporting organs for transplant. We typically move animals by aircraft and have a heavy-hauling single engine Cherokee Six for that purpose.

Generally animal delivery flights are uneventful, and I enjoy the time in the cockpit, but there have been a few sphincter-clenching moments. One summer we had a contract with the Kansas City Zoo to set up one of our live reptile exhibitions. The zoo had lined up print and television interviews for a Friday morning and wanted the reptiles in their habitats for Saturday's grand opening. It was critical that I get there on time. The annual inspection on our airplane was due to run out at the end of May, and our planned departure date was the 25th of the month. I reminded my mechanic about the approaching deadline, and he assured me the inspection would be done. When he finally pulled the airplane into his shop on Monday the 24th, my worst fear was confirmed. He called to say the left landing gear needed a part that he couldn't get until the next day— departure delayed.

Chad and I carefully calculated the weight of each box and its live contents and re-checked the weight and balance for the aircraft. With two people, luggage, fuel, and 950 pounds of live reptiles, there was no room to spare. I had been watching the weather trends for days and it looked good from Pennsylvania to Kansas City. The mechanic called late Wednesday night to say the repair was done.

Early Thursday morning a long-time employee and friend, John Tolbert, helped me load the Six and secure the containers firmly to the airframe. John and I piled into the cockpit and took off. As always, I was prepared to land and sit out any severe weather we encountered along the way.

We made two fuel stops en route and had lunch in Muncie, Indiana before pushing west over Illinois. At our last fuel stop in Decatur, the weather briefer mentioned a line of heavy thunderstorms just south of our route and suggested we deviate slightly north to avoid them. Soon after we were airborne we began to see a wall of blackness off our left wing. There was no turbulence and I commented to John that our flight had been incredibly smooth. Little did I know, that was about to change. A hundred miles out from Kansas City, our storm scope began to show lightning activity to our left that confirmed what our eyes were seeing. Then a few storm cells popped up behind us to the right. Our path still looked fine, although my attention was now riveted on the weather.

Suddenly the storm scope bristled with a cluster of lightning strikes directly behind us, and we began to experience moderate turbulence. The air traffic controller radioed that there was also weather ahead, and we might experience a smoother ride by heading 30 degrees left. That contradicted what the weather briefer had told us, but meteorological conditions change rapidly and I took the controller's advice. Things got worse fast. At 6,000 feet, we found ourselves in very rough conditions. The airplane pitched forward and rolled violently. I reduced power, hoping the wings weren't going to come off. Boiling black clouds surrounded us. I fought to keep the attitude of the Cherokee as steady as possible as we were thrust upward, then suddenly dropped 1,500 feet at a time, in a matter of seconds. The plane nosed into a dive, then seconds later I was pushing the yoke forward to avoid a stall. Lightning flashed. The controller noticed our erratic altitude and cleared us for anything between 6,000 and 8,000 feet—more if we needed it.

The Cherokee powered on and I kept it straight and level as best I could, focusing on the instrument panel and ignoring what was happening outside the thin aluminum hull. My passenger, John, held on for dear life and, to his credit, did not panic. After what seemed an eternity—probably 20 minutes—of very tough flying, we emerged from the worst of it 70 miles south of Kansas City. We made a circuitous route along the southwestern side, well clear of the mountain of black clouds, turned north, and approached Wheeler Downtown Airport from the west, still jostling about in rough air but grateful to be out of the storm.

As we taxied to the ramp and tied down, a Kansas City Zoo van was waiting for us. An hour later at the zoo we anxiously unpacked the reptiles unsure whether they had come through the experience alive. They seemed no worse for the wear.

And John? I was sure he would opt to return to Pennsylvania by bus, and I wouldn't have blamed him. But as we crawled out of the cockpit and planted our feet on terra firma, he said that if we survived that experience, he'd fly anywhere with me. Or I think that's what he said. Maybe that's what I wanted to hear. In the years since, we have put in a lot of time in that Cherokee together.

CHAPTER 12
Great Escapes and Close Calls

WORKING WITH LIVE animals always involves a degree of uncertainty. For many years Reptiland displayed baboons during the summers. We usually borrowed the animals from Bucknell University's research colony. But in the summer of 1982, we borrowed two adult female Hamadryas baboons—one of them carrying a newborn—from Rick Hahn at Catoctin Wildlife Park in Maryland.

An otherwise exceptional teenage employee and family friend, Dave Osman, forgot to snap the padlock after cleaning their exhibit at Reptiland. Before long, three baboons were running loose. A short time later they returned to their habitat on their own, deciding, apparently, that life was better there than roaming the countryside. The second time Dave made the same mistake, it was different; the baboons were gone for eleven days. They initially ran across US Route 15, onto the property of the Allenwood Federal Penitentiary. Newspaper reporters loved the story and tracked our progress, or lack of it, in locating the escapees. I called Rick Hahn to say he might receive a phone call from a reporter about his escaped baboons. Rick's response was immediate, "They're not my baboons. The moment they escaped, they became your baboons."

The telephone rang constantly. Someone would report having seen the baboons, and I would grab a tranquilizer gun and race to the scene—always too late. On the rare occasion I did catch a glimpse of the animals, they quickly ran out of tranquilizer-gun range. But there seemed to be a pattern to their movements. They were consistently seen in one of three locations—they had established a home range. Neighbors thought it was amusing to spot them in their gardens, on their front porches, or in nearby trees. I knew it was only a matter of time until the baboons discovered an open window and got into a home, where they could cause a lot of damage. Homeowners would quickly lose their sense of humor.

Imaginations ran wild. One man, who lived more than 20 miles away, phoned to say he had just seen my baboons. They had been sighted within a mile of Reptiland the day before, so I was skeptical. He insisted, "They're black with long tails, right?" No. I didn't know what he had seen, but they weren't baboons. He responded, "Well damn, what the hell did I see?"

We realized that the tranquilizer-gun approach was not going to work, so I borrowed a cannon net from the Pennsylvania Game Commission. Three small cannons with projectiles are attached to a net and, when detonated, shoot the net in an arc over the quarry. The Game Commission used canon nets to catch wild turkeys; we hoped they would work on baboons.

Of the three places the elusive primates had been spotted, one was the backyard of a kindly older woman, who allowed us to pile overripe fruit as bait on her lawn. We carefully aimed the cannons, retreated to a small nearby shed, and waited. Hour after boring hour passed with only flies attracted to the pile of fruit. By mid-afternoon we nearly dozed off in the heat, but suddenly there was a baboon at the fruit. It was a lone female. I couldn't see the female with the baby, but I knew we had to get at least one animal, so I touched off the cannons. Boom—the cannons exploded in unison, and the net sailed over the baboon. We had her, and, just outside the net, the second female appeared with her baby. She screamed and bounded along the perimeter of the net, concerned for her trapped partner. Dave deftly lifted a corner of the net, and, in her confusion, she ran under it. Sometimes things do work out as planned. We got out of the baboon business after that, but we've had a few close calls with reptiles too. Escapes in cars and planes were the most harrowing.

One day, having just finished a lecture at a school in southern New Jersey, I loaded my boxes of reptiles into my small Cherokee 140 and flew north toward Albany, New York. The boxes were stacked on the back seat except for one large one, containing an eleven-foot reticulated python. That box was on the passenger seat to my right, too large for the cramped rear seats. Somewhere south of the Catskills, I realized that the snake had popped off the lid and was pouring out of the box to explore the cockpit. It was reasonably tame, but pythons are quite strong, and I was alone without an autopilot. I flew the plane with my left hand, while frantically trying to stuff the snake's reluctant bulk back into the box with my right. Just about the time I thought I had succeeded, the snake would surge forth again, and I had to start all over. Finally, I was able to keep him contained just long enough to slam the lid shut. I noticed the bolt at one end had torn through the plastic lip of the box, so I held the lid firmly with my right hand until I could tell the snake was no longer pushing. I convinced myself it had settled down and released my grip.

A few minutes later the lid opened again. This time more than half the snake emerged from the box in a quick, fluid motion. It crawled into the rudder controls on the floor of the plane. While cursing my stupidity for relaxing, I grabbed the fore part of the snake and shoved it back into the box. Somehow I managed to retain control of the aircraft, get the python entirely into the box, and secure the lid—this time I held the lid on with my right hand and made a quick landing at Hudson, New York. I borrowed some duct tape from the fixed base operator, and the rest of the flight was uneventful.

On a flight to Houston, a four-foot water monitor—a close relative and smaller version of the Komodo dragon—escaped its traveling box. I had just taken off from a fuel stop at a small airport in Mississippi. Out of the corner of my eye I caught a movement, as the monitor lizard made its way between the two front seats of the Cherokee Six. There was no immediate danger, but I had no way to get him back into his container, which was out of reach at the very rear of the cargo hold. When I landed in Houston, the flight line crew was startled to see a long-tongued lizard staring at them from the airplane window.

One snake escape stands out from the rest. For more than a decade, I traveled frequently to sport and travel expositions in the Midwest during the off-season to supplement Reptiland's income. These shows sell space to vendors of outdoor equipment and owners of hunting and fishing lodges to display their products and services to hunters and fishermen. I was hired to set up wall exhibits—a series of reptile habitats—to help attract people to the show. It was tough work, and usually I took a long-term employee, Mike Fetterman, to help. We would open the tour in Cedar Rapids, move to La Crosse, on to Duluth, and end the month-long tour in Omaha. We transported the animals in a van and took turns driving all night to get from one city to the next.

About three o'clock one cold February morning, Mike was driving on I-80 near Davenport, Iowa, while I slept. We towed a trailer that contained all the exhibit components and transported the reptiles inside the heated van with us. Mike had packed the animals hurriedly and, as it turned out, not too securely. As he clicked off mile after boring mile in the cold darkness, he felt what he thought was a shift in his seatbelt position and reached down to adjust it. I was awakened when he yelped, "What the hell?" The next thing I heard was, "Snake!" Seconds later, "King cobra!" Now I was wide awake.

This giant cobra—the largest species of venomous snake—was crawling across his lap, and he had grabbed it, not his seat belt, at mid-body. To Mike's credit, he didn't panic. He kept the van and trailer moving straight ahead and decelerated safely. Pushing as far back in his seat as possible, elbows held high, not knowing exactly where the snake's head was in the darkness, he stopped the vehicle along the interstate. I grabbed a snake hook—never leave home without one—and pulled the snake off him. The cobra made no effort at aggression, and together we put it back into its box. For the next three hours, we reconstructed what had happened and laughed nervously all the way to Cedar Rapids. We could just imagine pulling into a hospital in the middle of Iowa in February and telling a doctor: "I've just been bitten by a king cobra." To which the doctor might respond: "Don't worry, sir, we don't have cobras in Iowa."

One year, Reptiland traded a group of emus, Australian birds that were quite valuable at the time, for two 12-foot alligators at Florida's St. Augustine Alligator Farm. I called Arthur Jones for advice about how best to move the alligators. He emphasized the necessity to build compartments to prevent such large, powerful animals from shifting position during transit. He had once hauled a number of large alligators that were loose in a rental trailer. At one point, all the alligators moved to the back of the trailer, causing the rear of his car to lift off the pavement, which made steering "problematic." We took Arthur's advice, built two stalls of 2x4s and 3/4" plywood in a trailer we owned, and Chad, John Tolbert, and I headed to Florida with the emus. We stopped first at Arthur's ranch in Ocala, where he gave us a large rope net he had used when he flew 85 baby elephants from Africa in his Boeing 707. We would need the net to lift the 800-pound alligators into their new habitat, upon our return to Reptiland. Then we drove to St. Augustine to catch and load the alligators.

The manager of the Alligator Farm, Bill Puckett, assured us there were approximately eighty 12-foot male alligators in one large enclosure, and we could have our pick. Along with the Alligator Farm staff, we measured alligator after alligator and, to everyone's surprise, we couldn't find a single 12-footer. No one was trying to deceive us: it's nearly impossible, even for experts, to accurately judge the length of an adult crocodilian. Due to their bulk, big crocs look longer than they are. We finally chose two of the biggest alligators—one measured 11' 3" and the other 11' 8". They were impressive reptiles, and the next challenge was to get ropes on them.

With help from Alligator Farm employees, we noosed and dragged the giants to a nearby tree, where we tied them securely. One danger, aside from the possibility of having a limb torn off by the powerful jaws, is being struck by the heavy bony skull, as the animal thrashes from side to side. Getting hit on a leg would be equivalent to being hit with a sledgehammer. After considerable effort, we taped the jaws without injury to the animals or us, pulled the giants up the ramp of our trailer, and coaxed them into their separate stalls.

As we drove north out of Florida, we could occasionally feel slight fishtailing from the trailer. When we stopped for fuel, just over the Georgia line, we discovered why. Both alligators had destroyed their stalls and were moving about freely inside the thin fiberglass walls of the trailer. One had torn the tape off its snout. In the darkness there wasn't much we could do, so we closed the door and continued up the interstate. Over the next twelve hours, we felt movement from the rear, each time wondering whether one or both of the gators would simply walk through the trailer walls— which they could easily have done—and plop onto the highway. As luck would have it, the alligators stayed inside the trailer. When we arrived at Reptiland, we let them walk down the trailer ramp onto the rope net, and a local backhoe operator each alligator over the wall of their new home and safely into their pool.

Working with animals is never entirely without risk, but we take safety seriously and have transported thousands of animals without incident. Stories of things going wrong are the only ones fun enough to read about. They represent the most extreme and memorable cases, over a period of 50 years; not the everyday happenings at a modern zoo.

Chad Peeling on a radio appearance lecturing about venomous snakes. Photo courtesy Backyard Broadcasting

Elliot Peeling putting the finishing touches on a fiberglass tree in a frog habitat.

Chris Bergesen-Peeling directed marketing and gift store operations for 25 years.

National television appearances rarely offered the chance to do much educating, but put Reptiland in front of huge audiences. Top to bottom: *The Tonight Show with Jay Leno*, *Late Night with Conan O'Brien*, with Thane Maynard (the Ninety-Second Naturalist) on *The Saturday Early Show*.

More television antics.

A snake in the class

Slither   Press-Enterprise/Bill Hughes
Students at Huntington Mills Elementary School stretch to touch a python wrapped around the neck of Clyde Peeling, owner of Reptileland near Allenwood, Friday afternoon after a PTO sponsored the assembly.

BOB LAMB

Sports show should be wild

Amazon Rain Forest exhibit promises to be creepy, crawly

It's Hisssssssstory

CLYDE PEELING'S LOVE OF SNAKES—
BIG SNAKES, LITTLE SNAKES, LOTS OF SNAKES—
GOES BACK TO CATCHING A HOGNOSED SNAKE AT SCOUT CAMP.

BOA, OH, BOA!

BY ALISON DELSITE

STOP BY FOR A
SLITHER

A SNAKE-NECK TURTLE swims around in its tank in a Reptiland display.

Cold-blooded creatures await at Clyde Peeling's Reptiland

Lizards, Tortoises, Boas – Oh My!

After feeding an apple to "Pepe," Clyde Peeling rubs the tortoise Aldabra's neck while visitors look on at Clyde Peeling's Reptiland near Allenwood. "Pepe" is indigenous to an atoll in the Indian Ocean. Peeling got the tortoise in 1969 when it weighed only five pounds. "Pepe" now weighs more than 300 pounds.

Snakebitten since youth

Peeling's attraction to reptiles becomes popular Valley attraction

Up close and perssssssonal

Reptiland opens program focusing on venomous creatures

One of our traveling exhibitions, *Geckos-Tails to Toepads*, installed in a museum gallery.

Elliot Peeling (front left) and his team of exhibit fabricators after finishing construction of the traveling exhibition, *Frogs–A Chorus of Colors.*

Vagabond baboons spotted, but flee again

ALLENWOOD — Clyde Peeling had the best chance yet Sunday to capture his escapees. Two of them were up in a tree about a quarter mile south of Reptiland in Gregg Township.

Peeling's wife had cornered two of the three missing baboons. She got someone in the search party to phone her husband, and he hurried to the site, but he moved a little too fast.

"I blew it. I thought I was walking slow enough towards the tree, but when I got within eyesight I scared the mother and her baby off," said Peeling, owner of Reptiland on Route 15.

"They were in a tree at one of the places where they have been hanging around. If my wife knew how to shoot a tranquilizer gun, we would have had those two," Peeling said.

He said the mother ape walked up to his wife Sunday. "I think they are afraid of men," he said.

The third baboon, another female, was seen Sunday morning crossing Route 15 just south of Reptiland.

The baboons, on loan from the Catoctin Mountain Zoo in Maryland, have been spotted several times last week within a mile of Reptiland.

Monkey business in Allenwood

By Paul Boyer
staff reporter

ALLENWOOD — Allenwood residents had better keep their bananas under lock and key. Three unusual escapees might be interested in a snack.

The escapees, three baboons, loped away Sunday afternoon from Peeling's Reptiland, a specialized zoo on Route 15 in northern Union County, according to Clyde Peeling, the owner.

"My keeper forgot to padlock their cage. It doesn't take a baboon, which is very intelligent, very long to figure out how to remove the lock," Peeling said.

He said the two adults and a baby, on loan from the Catoctin Mountain Zoo in Maryland, crossed Route 15 and disappeared into the woods near another pen — the federal prison farm.

Baboons are about the size of a collie and weigh about 50 pounds.

The animals, valued at $300 to $500 each, were spotted Sunday night hanging out in tree between Route 15 and the prison farm fence. But the baboons had swung away before the long arm of the law could reach them.

Peeling said the baboons were sighted between Reptiland and Allenwood Tuesday night in a child's tree house. But the hairy visitors again fled before his staff arrived.

"They won't attack anyone. They probably will run from you. They are afraid of people. I don't think they will go very far. Some people I talked to who are familiar with baboons said they would probably stay within a mile radius of here," Peeling said.

Peeling is quick to answer the telephone. "Every time it rings, I think it's going to be someone who spotted them."

Until then, the baboons will be free to monkey around.

(Daily Item — Paul Boyer)

Rocket net did the job

Clyde Peeling examines the device that enabled him to catch three baboons that escaped from his Reptiland on July 11. The canisters contain a net which is ejected by small rockets. The apes were returned to captivity Thursday after they were snared in a backyard along Route 15 north of Allenwood, not far from Peeling's establishment.

2   Williamsport Sun-Gazette, Thursday, July 22, 1982

LATEST WEAPON in Clyde Peeling's hunt for his three runaway baboons is this rocket trap on loan from the Pennsylvania Game Commission. David G. Osman, zoo-keeper at Reptiland, near Allenwood, inspects the contraption yesterday. He is holding a tranquilizer dart gun. The three apes got out of their unlocked cage on July 11 and have been eluding capture ever since. Peeling said a resident of the area near the zoo reported the baboons were inspecting the trap about an hour after this picture was taken. "We went back down, but they had evaporated, of course," Peeling stated. The rockets will hopefully throw the net over the baboons when Peeling or his assistants trigger it from a nearby blind. Food has been placed nearby to attract the baboons.

When three baboons escaped from Reptiland in 1987, it sparked an 11-day spate of media coverage (and stress) until they were safely recaptured.

Moving a massive American alligator into its habitat after a long drive from St. Augustine Alligator Farm in Florida required heavy equipment and gentle maneuvering.

John Strawbridge has influenced the style and philosophy of Reptiland since its inception. Circa 2013.

Jeff Cook started his zoo career at Reptiland in the mid-1970s and returned to our staff 30 years later.

John Tolbert joined our team in 1999, just as we were entering the traveling exhibits business. His sensitivity to animals and plants helped refine our exhibit style.

Debbie and John Behler, of the Wildlife Conservation Society (Bronx Zoo), encouraged our evolving professionalism and AZA accreditation.

George Craig (left) captured the largest crocodile ever exhibited in North America. He began as a hide hunter in the 1960s, but came to love big crocs, and has cared for them at his facility in Australia for more than 30 years. Circa 2005.

Capturing giant crocs without hurting the animal (or getting hurt) is not for the timid. George Craig stands astride a giant estuarine crocodile in Papua, New Guinea. Circa 1966.

This state-of-the-art Komodo dragon habitat opened at Reptiland in 2013.

The entrance of the *Island Giants* building at Reptiland where Komodo dragons and Aldabra tortoises are housed.

The Reptiland front entrance building—renovated and enlarged in 2013.

The Peeling family 2004. Back row L to R: Elliot, Chad, Dianne, Clyde
Front row L toR: Chris holding Evan, Pierce, and Whitney

CHAPTER 13
Reptiland - the Future

I HAVE BEEN FORTUNATE to surround myself with people more clever than me, to paraphrase Andrew Carnegie's epitaph. Reptiland has attracted many talented individuals who, in small or large measure, became part of our extended family. Their numbers—hundreds over the years—prohibit mentioning them all, but they have been instrumental in making Reptiland what it is today. A few have been with us for decades. As of this writing, our team numbers about 40 professionals with expertise extending to many disciplines—animal care, exhibit design, art, marketing, retail, media production, and horticulture.

As Reptiland passes its fiftieth anniversary I look back at the philosophical changes we have undergone and how they portend our future, and the future of zoos in general. I started Reptiland thinking we were in the animal business. A half century later, I am convinced we are in the education business. Informal education to be sure—most people visit zoos to be entertained—but the animals are the hook that allows us to capture an audience. Once we have visitors' attention, we have an opportunity and obligation to inspire wonder and teach them something about the animals they came to see. And we have to do it in a way that is fun.

Do zoos matter? It's a fair question, and the answer is yes; but only if we fulfill our missions. The bulk of the human population now lives in cities with little access to nature. Television is fine, but nothing evokes empathy and emotional connection with wildlife like experiencing a real living creature. Done properly, zoos connect people with diverse forms of animal life, communicate pivotal scientific ideas, and emphasize that all life is inextricably interwoven. I believe education is our primary mission.

Zoological institutions also invest millions of dollars annually to support field conservation programs around the world—work that wouldn't be possible otherwise. And modern zoos are now working cooperatively to manage sustainable populations of animals in captivity. Guided by detailed pedigrees and statistical breeding models, population managers work to preserve the genetic diversity of wild animals in zoo populations. For a few species, zoos have become "survival islands," the last refuge before total extinction. I do not pretend that zoos can save more than a tiny handful of species by reintroducing captive animals to the wild, but we can cooperate with academic scientists, field biologists, governments, and local people to facilitate meaningful environmental change. And most important, zoos can galvanize the energy and support of visitors— particularly the young—toward a realistic conservation ethic.

Preserving genetic diversity in captive populations is a daunting task, requiring space, staff, and significant financial resources. Zoos can't do it alone, but there are thousands of private individuals who specialize in and breed many species of reptiles and amphibians in captivity. David and Tracy Barker, best known for their work with pythons, refer to these collective populations as *The Invisible Ark*; invisible because they are not part of any organized entity and are largely unknown and unnoticed by most citizens. Zoos need the cooperation and assistance of the invisible ark to increase the size of managed populations and bring the maximum resources to bear. Private owners of captive populations could to be brought into the fold and made active partners of Species Survival Plans (SSPs). Their animals could be genetically managed in the same studbooks with zoo populations to ensure long-term sustainability. Many private breeders select for unusual morphological colors and patterns. These 'morphs' have no value to zoo populations, but breeders who also maintain "normal" populations could cooperate with SSPs to ensure long-term access to genetically diverse animals.

Zoos aren't perfect, but they have taken considerable unfair criticism over the past few decades, particularly from the animal rights community. The most vocal animal rights groups are fundamentally against keeping animals in captivity and guided by people with emotional, rather than rational, motivations. The disconnect between animal rights groups and zoos is both philosophical and practical. Zoo professionals care passionately about individual animals (why else would one spend a career working with them?), but zoo animals are not our pets. Our charge is to manage populations of animals and to conserve biodiversity. We continually balance doing what's best for the population with providing quality of life for individual animals. In some ways we are closer to farmers than to pet owners, and there are times when we must euthanize animals as food for other species or to thin a herd. It's a question of focusing on the forest or the trees.

Animal rights activists tug at the public heartstrings, but contribute nothing to solving the crisis of declining biodiversity around the world. Our friend Jack Hanna, Director Emeritus of the Columbus Zoo and Aquarium, said it best when he was a guest on HBO's Real Time with Bill Maher. Maher, a passionate animal rights advocate, challenged Jack on the value of zoos. Jack responded by asking Bill how many dollars are contributed annually to wildlife conservation by People for the Ethical Treatment of Animals (PETA). Bill didn't know. The answer, of course, is none. PETA, and likeminded groups, are concerned about individual animals, not the accelerating loss of species to extinction. Zoos, in contrast, contribute more than $160 million a year to wildlife conservation, supporting 2,600 conservation projects in 130 countries. And these numbers exclude conservation education, our greatest strength.

If zoos have failed in any aspect of their collective missions, it has been science education—specifically evolution. The United States is unique among developed nations in the proportion of citizens who live in denial of organic evolution, a scientific principle that has been well established for more than 150 years. Surveys show that roughly half the U.S. population believes that man and animals were created in their current form.

One day a number of years ago, a church van pulled into the Reptiland parking lot. The minister, who doubled as driver, led his flock of children into the entrance building and up to the admission counter, preparing to visit the zoo. The lettering on the van advertised that it belonged to a Christian fundamentalist church, and I thought I'd give the minister fair warning that his students would be exposed to the subject of evolution in our interpretive graphics and lecture demonstration. He gave me a patronizing smile, put a kindly hand on my shoulder, and told me not to be concerned. "Our kids know better," he said. I've heard this sort of thing for 50 years and it's baffling to me. The enormous weight of evidence from disparate fields makes the history of life's evolution as undeniable as gravity, and it is impossible to teach anything about the biological world without it.

In general, museums do a much better job presenting the subject of evolution than zoos, even though zoos are ideally positioned to do it. After all, visitors come face to face with living, breathing examples of evolutionary diversity. Evolution is axiomatic to biologists, yet the subject is often soft-pedaled in zoo education programs for fear of upsetting donors, inflaming local politicians, or risking bad press. I know of an aquarium in the Bible Belt where the staff is prohibited from even mentioning the "E" word in public areas.

There is a never-ending effort by some fundamentalist groups to cast doubt and prevent schools and other institutions from teaching evolution. In 2005, for example, vocal religious fundamentalists in Oklahoma pushed the Tulsa Zoo to include Intelligent Design, a euphemism for creationism, in its interpretive graphics. The issue created a firestorm of press stories, but the zoo bravely refused to capitulate. Just as the Scopes Trial of 1925 unnerved many biology teachers about teaching evolution in classrooms for more than thirty years, media storms like the one in Tulsa instill fear in the hearts of many zoo directors.

As Bill Cosby said, "I don't know the key to success, but the key to failure is trying to please everybody." If zoos dodge the scientific underpinnings of biology for political expediency, it will come back to bite us in the form of an even less informed citizenry. Reptiland is located in a religiously conservative part of the country and relies exclusively on visitor-generated revenue, yet we interpret evolution at every opportunity. Although a handful of visitors have voiced opposition over the years, I've seen no evidence that it has had a negative impact on our business. I hope that efforts like ours and those in Tulsa will become more common.

Probably the most frequent refrain I've heard throughout my career is, "I hate snakes." I suspect what that really means is, "I fear snakes." Whichever the case, snakes are surely among the most reviled animals. Sometimes this fear degenerates into near panic. Forty years ago an eleven-foot reticulated python briefly escaped from Reptiland, and I made a point to go door to door notifying our neighbors. I reassured them it was not large enough to pose any danger. Within an hour of spreading the word, I received a phone call from a concerned farmer. "Is it true," he wanted to know, "that you've got a snake loose capable of swallowing a water buffalo?"

A bigger problem with irrational fears is that they sometimes drive public policy. The area in and around the Everglades of South Florida is overrun with invasive species—exotic plants, fish, iguanas, caimans, boas, and other tropical organisms that have established populations. Invasive species often out-compete native wildlife and pose a serious threat to biodiversity. Within the last decade, a breeding population of Burmese pythons, snakes native to Southeast Asia and capable of growing to 16 feet, was discovered in the region. Their release in the accommodating subtropics around Miami, probably the doing of disreputable animal dealers, has created an undeniable threat to wildlife. Adult pythons are big enough to tackle waterfowl, small alligators, and even a newborn deer. Like all species invasions, this one demanded a swift regional response. Unfortunately, it elicited something entirely different.

The reaction to pythons in South Florida escalated beyond anything rational, and prompted a regulatory response completely out of proportion (and unhelpful) to the problem. Media outlets lapped up the story of big pythons on the loose, inventing a misleading threat to humans (even giant snakes do not include people in their diets). In a misguided effort to steer federal funds their way, Florida officials tendered bills in Congress and petitioned the US Fish & Wildlife Service to add giant constrictors to its list of "injurious wildlife," restricting interstate transport of the animals without a federal permit.

Ken Salazar, then Secretary of the Interior, took advantage of the PR opportunity and held a press conference announcing his agency's intent to regulate the interstate movement of pythons and boas—a bold move, prior to undertaking the required scientific and economic review process. An easier political win could hardly be imagined: do something to protect the environment while clamping down on snakes, which nobody loves. Who could possibly complain?

The problem is that tropical pythons do not pose a threat to the vast majority of the U.S.—the sub-tropical climate of South Florida is uniquely vulnerable. Parlaying a regional problem into federal regulation adds a stifling burden to the operation of zoos and other legitimate wildlife organizations nation-wide and fails to address the real crisis. To satisfy the procedural requirement for scientific review, a study was undertaken by the US Geological Survey to assess the threat of invasion by giant snakes for the rest of the nation. It was an academic analysis based on narrow data, and it led to some astounding conjecture. The study suggested that Burmese pythons could, with moderate global warming, expand their populations north as far as Delaware and Southern Pennsylvania and west along the southern half of the U.S. Professionals who have kept the species for decades recognized that the study was deeply flawed—even with brief exposure to temperatures in the 40s and 50s, large tropical snakes succumb to lethal respiratory infections. But the Interior Secretary had announced his intentions *a priori*, and conflicting information was set aside. The fix was in, and the pythons were regulated.

We must find a way, as a nation, to respond effectively to environmental crises without exacerbating unnecessary regulatory burdens. Invasive species are an undeniable threat to biodiversity, but the threats to one region must not be extrapolated to the whole continent, buoyed by irrational fears. The best solution is a proactive and educated citizenry. Reactive overregulation is a lazy and costly political expedient and threatens the ability of organizations like Reptiland to function.

In spite of the obstacles facing zoos, I remain optimistic about the future. In the United States, more people visit zoos each year than attend all professional sporting events combined. As E.O. Wilson points out in his book *Creation*, "People like other species." Wild places are rapidly disappearing, and the cost of air travel to visit the vestiges of intact nature may someday be prohibitive to all but the very wealthy. People need to connect with wild animals, and zoos may be the only option.

CHAPTER 14
Crocodiles and Dragons

AS I WRITE, REPTILAND is working to create an ambitious traveling exhibition called *Crocs—Ancient Predators in a Modern World*. This exhibition features wonderful life-sized models of crocodilians, live specimens, interactive exhibits, and a guided tour by our friend Kent Vliet, an expert on crocodilians who acts as "digital curator".

One feature of the project—a spectacular model of Gomek, the biggest crocodile ever exhibited in the Western Hemisphere—began to crystallize in 2007, when we were installing another traveling exhibition in Ft. Lauderdale, Florida. I flew as far as Saint Augustine the first leg of the trip, stashed coolers of live frogs safely in my motel room for the night, and headed to the St. Augustine Alligator Farm, which was hosting a crocodilian workshop for zoo professionals. The place was swarming with croc experts.

As I entered the zoo grounds, Alligator Farm owner David Drisdale emerged through a side gate and asked if I knew his friend George Craig, the man who captured Gomek nearly 40 years earlier. I had heard plenty about George from Arthur Jones, who was always fascinated by giant crocs. George and I immediately hit it off, and we spent the entire evening talking about women, crocodiles, and Arthur. I determined to spend more time with George and promised to visit his place on Green Island, fifteen miles off the coast of Cairns, Australia.

The very next year Chad, Elliot, and I flew to Australia to film interviews with a number of crocodilian biologists and George, a former crocodile hunter who had come to love the animals he once killed for a living. George is fascinating because his life embodies a broad change in societal views toward crocodiles in Australia and New Guinea. As a young man, he made his living shooting crocs for the hide market and viewed them as an inexhaustible resource. He and his wife, Shirley, made a home in Daru at the mouth of the Fly River in New Guinea, and, for sixteen years, George made expeditions 500 miles up and down the Fly, killing crocs and trading for skins with the local hunters. As the years passed, he could see that unrestrained hunting was not sustainable.

George told us that when he killed his first giant crocodile, he felt terrible. The animal had guarded the mouth of a tributary to the Fly River for, perhaps, 80 years and, in an instant, George had ended its life. Yet he could see that the days of mega-sized crocs were numbered—the biggest were regularly becoming entangled in fishing nets and drowning. George decided to try to catch some of the giants alive.

He devised a technique to bait a small grappling hook with the remains of a giant fruit bat and tie it to a floating buoy on a long line. He placed the bait in an area a big croc was known to frequent and left for the night. The hope was that the hook would snag the croc's lower jaw and not be swallowed, which would mean almost certain death. George and his crew would locate a hooked croc by following the buoy, then gently pulling the line until the croc surfaced. George would pull his skiff alongside the croc (the boat little bigger than the crocodile) and thrust a tiny barbed harpoon, attached to a rope, under the armored scutes of its neck. The barb penetrated far enough to provide a sturdy grip, without injuring the animal. On impact the croc would go crazy, spinning wildly in the black water, wrapping itself in the rope. George played the animal patiently until it became tired. After hours of fighting, he pulled the exhausted crocodile to the skiff and roped it to one or more long poles. Muscular New Guineans winched the animals, some of which weighed nearly 2,000 pounds, onto the deck of George's larger diesel powered boat. They covered the croc with wet burlap to prevent overheating on the long trip downstream to holding facilities George had prepared in Daru. George captured seven giant crocodiles in this manner in the 1960s.

By 1971, New Guinea was in turmoil, about to gain independence from Australia and unsafe for outsiders. George wanted to get his family out. He purchased a small public aquarium on Green Island, just off the Australian mainland, added large pools for his crocs, and moved everything out of New Guinea. When Arthur Jones read about this fellow who had the biggest crocodiles in the world, he was determined to seek him out and try to purchase a big one. Arthur, his young wife Terry, ex-football player Dick Butkus, and a copilot flew to Australia in Arthur's Cessna Citation.

When Arthur and his entourage arrived at Green Island, George's wife, Shirley, announced that there was an obnoxious man in the gift shop demanding to see him. Arthur said he wanted to buy George's biggest crocodile, but George explained he did not sell his crocodiles to just anyone. Upon leaving hours later, Arthur pushed a wad of money into George's hand and insisted he come to Florida to see how Arthur kept his crocodiles. After Arthur left, George buried the money in a jar behind his house. Months later he decided to take Arthur up on his offer to visit, but George had forgotten exactly where he buried the money—after excavating a big part of the yard, he found it.

George visited Florida, and he and Arthur became close friends, remaining so until Arthur's death in 2007. George eventually sold Arthur his second largest saltwater crocodile—the eighteen-foot Gomek. Arthur later sent Gomek to the St. Augustine Alligator

Farm, where the croc lived out the rest of its life. George kept the remainder of his giant crocodiles and continues to care for them at Marineland Melanesia on Green Island.

George Craig is one of the last of the authentic crocodile hunters. But he is also a kind and conscientious man who has spent more than half of his adult life caring for the world's largest crocodiles. He knows each of his animals intimately and has a deep understanding of saltwater crocodiles, both in the wild and in captivity. At the end of our interview he said modestly, "Yeah, I know a thing or two about crocs. I know they'll eat you if they can!"

In the fall of 2010, our crocodile exhibition project was unexpectedly put on hiatus by a call from the Los Angeles Zoo. For years, Reptiland had been on a waiting list to join the Komodo dragon Species Survival Plan (SSP) as soon as animals were available, and the LA Zoo had just hatched a clutch of eggs. "Do you still want dragons?" they asked. We did, and suddenly found ourselves designing facilities for two young lizards that would quickly become giants. Komodo dragons are intelligent and active predators—the big cats of the reptile world—they need lots of space, blistering temperatures, and intense sunlight. Chad worked on facility designs, and Elliot and his crew began re-shaping an entire section of the zoo to accommodate a new building. An ordinary structure was out of the question: recreating the dragons' natural habitat in Central Pennsylvania required heavily insulated double block walls, a living roof with large skylights, under-soil radiant heat, and a computer-controlled environmental system. As often happens with new projects, one thing leads to another. Two years and two million dollars later, our dragons were introduced to their new surroundings in June 2013. The facility is a world-class center for endangered giant reptiles.

CHAPTER 15

Conclusion

IN SOME WAYS THIS book is the story of my life. But it's also about the birth of an institution and the contributions of many people who have enabled it to survive and grow. Through its years of slow development—from just another roadside attraction to the era of major traveling exhibitions—my wife Dianne has been supportive and tolerated more than should be expected of any partner.

I sometimes ask myself what I hoped to achieve when I started Reptiland. Did I really think I'd get rich in the zoo business? I certainly dreamed of success, but I think I knew I was choosing a lifestyle—not a road to wealth. I seldom walk through the zoo grounds now without hearing a compliment. A lady thanked me recently for realizing my dream so that her grandchildren could enjoy Reptiland. What more gratifying words could I ever hope to hear?

If people are familiar with the word "herpetologist," most would say that is what I am—someone who studies reptiles and amphibians. But I have never been comfortable with the label. I do not formally study herpetology in the lab or the field. I popularize the subject and interpret the work of ground-breaking scientists for a general audience. As a colleague on the advisory board to the Pennsylvania Fish and Boat Commission (the agency that regulates reptiles and amphibians in the Commonwealth) once quipped, "You may not be a herpetologist but you play one on TV." It got a laugh, but it's pretty close to the truth.

From humble beginnings in an unlikely location, Reptiland evolved into a specialized accredited zoological institution. It didn't happen by accident but luck certainly played a part. For me, luck included having a supportive wife and three kids who grew up with a work ethic, with two of them plus a daughter-in-law joining the business. I've also benefited from a network of employees, friends, and mentors who challenged my thinking and expanded my world view. For my part, it was tenacity, vision, and ego that kept me forging ahead during times when most sane businessmen would have packed it in. I'm not sure whether those traits are assets or curses—but here we are. In spite of the failures and roadblocks, I'd do it all over again. I love the Susquehanna River valleys and nearby mountains and have spent my life doing what I wanted to do.

Whether I represent success depends upon one's definition of the word, but I am certainly evidence that you can follow the unlikeliest of paths in life. My advice for anyone with a dream is that life is short: we only go around once. Don't let anyone talk you out of it.

ABOUT THE AUTHOR

Clyde Peeling became interested in reptiles at age twelve. As a teenager, growing up in rural Pennsylvania, he maintained a personal collection of live reptiles and worked at a private reptile zoo. In 1964 he opened Reptiland in Allenwood, Pennsylvania, beginning a life-long pursuit of his boyhood dream. What started as a small roadside zoo has evolved into a modern institution.

Clyde is a professional lecturer, private pilot, and active member of the zoological community. He has been a guest on many television shows including *The Tonight Show with Jay Leno, Late Night with Conan O'Brien, Live with Regis and Kathie Lee, The Jon Stewart Show, Real Life with Jane Pauley, The Today Show, ABC Wide World of Sports, To Tell the Truth* and others.

He lives with his wife near Reptiland in central Pennsylvania.

Made in the USA
Middletown, DE
11 April 2021